Behavioural Technical Analysis

An introduction to behavioural finance and its role in technical analysis

T0323012

By Paul V. Azzopardi

HARRIMAN HOUSE LTD

3A Penns Road
Petersfield
Hampshire
GU32 2EW
GREAT BRITAIN

Tel: +44 (0)1730 233870
Fax: +44 (0)1730 233880
Email: enquiries@harriman-house.com
Website: www.harriman-house.com

First published in Great Britain in 2010 by Harriman House.

978-1-905641-41-3

British Library Cataloguing in Publication Data
A CIP catalogue record for this book can be obtained from the British Library.

Printed in the UK by the CPI Group Antony Rowe, Chippenham

to Warren Paul and Marie Claire

Disclaimer

The information, analysis and strategies discussed in this book are provided for informational and education purposes only and should not be considered to be investment advice.

Readers should do their own independent research and seek professional advice before investing.

Readers should understand that there is a high degree of risk involved in trading securities and other financial instruments.

Facts mentioned in this book should be re-checked against official sources before investing.

Contents

Acknowledgements

The people who have helped with this book, directly or indirectly, are numerous and listing them all would be tedious (and generally meaningless) to the reader. But a few persons, in my life and in this project, stand above all the rest.

To my parents, Joseph and Pauline, and to my grandparents, Paul and Mary Grace Sammut, I owe oceans of gratitude for their love, good example and for always encouraging me to seek knowledge.

To my wife, Jennifer, invariably a source of encouragement and enthusiasm but always with an eye on an even keel.

To my project editor at Harriman House, Stephen Eckett, who has not only been patient and supportive over many months but who also did his best to make sure I wrote the book for others, not myself.

I would like to thank my readers for choosing to read this book. I hope you enjoy reading it as much as I enjoyed writing it.

If you have any comments or suggested improvements please email me at email@paulvazzopardi.com.

I have set up a website at www.behaviouraltechnicalanalysis.com to provide relevant links for this book, supporting material and occasional articles.

Paul V. Azzopardi

Ontario, Canada
October 31, 2009

Preface

In a sense, investors are be seen as living a life-long struggle against the randomness of market prices. For my part, I tried to make some sense of these utterly capricious but captivating markets by first becoming a certified accountant, in order to learn the language of business, and later immersing myself in as much investment theory as I could.

I therefore started from the trenches of fundamentals and was soon led to the mathematically elegant boulevards of efficient markets, the capital asset pricing model and option pricing theories. I found lots of stimuli but little satisfaction.

For quite a long while I compromised and worked on the assumption that if I did my homework and got the basics of the fundamentals right, I could then join the market with a diversified portfolio, watch over it, and hope for the best. I tried to improve on this basic setup with stop loss levels and, strategically, by trying to guess the next move. It sort of worked, on average, but I was far from happy with the results.

It was when I first read *Reminiscences of a Stock Operator*, Edwin Lefèvre's masterpiece based on the life of Jesse Livermore, that I realised fundamentals had *a* role to play – but not *the* role – and that the market had to be seen as having a life of its own, fuelled by sentiment. I realised that it was sentiment that made the market move and that this movement was evident in the footprints of price. Sentiment, furthermore, was nothing more than the collective psychology of the participants in the market. This potpourri of fundamentals, footprints and sentiment had to somehow show me the way.

At about the same time, in various articles, I came across references to Kahneman and Tversky's work on prospect theory and how they proposed that people often made use of rules of thumb, so-called heuristics, to make decisions in uncertain conditions. They were writing about such concepts as representativeness, availability, anchoring and adjustment. And what was I, and many other investors, doing if not deciding under uncertainty? Kahneman and Tversky's behavioural finance approach was using up-to-the-minute research techniques, drawn from psychology, economics, statistics and various other disciplines to try to get to the bottom of Livermore's market psychology. I felt this work went to the heart of the markets and I was hooked.

Decision making lies at the heart of investing and behavioural finance describes how people decide – it was clear to me that behavioural finance should be a core investment discipline. It also soon became evident to me that while fundamentals dealt with the day after tomorrow (if fed good data), I could only know what was happening now and what was likely to happen tomorrow by looking at price patterns on graphs. This led me to the realisation that sentiment and price patterns have to be observed most closely, with fundamentals and economic models as background. One other crucial thing is to collect evidence with statistics and quantitative techniques to make sure it is fact, and not myth, which is being studied. This re-focus changed my whole approach to investment.

As the turn of events in 2008 and 2009 showed, the nature of the market is that no one can have perpetual success and that each person involved in the markets is on the way to learning more. I hope, however, that this re-focus helps my readers to improve their performance as it helped me to improve mine.

The rise of behavioural finance

I am very pleased to note that technical analysis associations around the world are increasingly including market sentiment and investor psychology studies in their approved body of knowledge and course curricula as well as giving greater importance to evidence validated by statistical testing. Papers dealing with the behavioural finance aspects of technical analysis now feature in important conferences and awards.

Influential bodies such as the Market Technicians Association (USA), the Society of Technical Analysts (UK), the Canadian Society of Technical Analysts, the Australian Technical Analysts Association and the Technical Analysts Society (Singapore), as well as other similar associations around the world, are proactively including behavioural finance findings in approved research.

The Technical Analyst magazine in the UK, for example, regularly holds conferences, training and other events, and has started a series of behavioural finance seminars for "traders and investment managers looking to exploit market inefficiencies using market psychology." The 2008 seminar included speakers on prospect theory, over- and under-reaction, herding and using behavioural finance in value investing. These and similar initiatives around the world augur new horizons in finance and securities trading which have the potential to transform the way we approach markets.

Firms providing investor relations services are now analysing shareholders not only by type (institution, mutual fund, individual, etc) but also by style of investment management and whether there are buy-side or sell-side pressures amongst different shareholding classes. Behavioural finance, therefore, is influencing not only investment decision making but also the relationships between corporations and their owners.

The objectives of this book

This book has three main objectives. My first objective is to introduce behavioural finance to investors in a practical, interesting and structured manner. After the introductory Part One, giving some background to behavioural finance, in Part Two I have presented the main concepts of behavioural finance so that the reader is provided with a grounding in the whole subject area.

My second objective, as important as the first, is to try and give some pointers as to how one might attempt to combine the rapidly developing but rather new field of behavioural finance with the insights offered by technical analysis, which has been around ever since markets as we know them began to take shape. This combination I call *behavioural technical analysis.*

I feel that the mutual pollination of behavioural finance and technical analysis can lead to new and stimulating vistas. I hope that the logic of fusing the two disciplines, and testing the hypotheses generated with objective observation and modern quantitative techniques, will provide impetus to further research in this area and, importantly, create new ways of making money.

My third objective is that this book be of practical value to the investor, helping them to find a way to make money. This book does not contain a secret formula which enables you to acquire great wealth on the market in a few months by dedicating a few minutes a day. Instead, at the end of each chapter in Part Two there is a summary section, discussing how the behavioural finance area just explored can be used by investors. This is extended further in Part Three, where I examine the behavioural finance concepts supporting three strategies which technical analysts have utilised over the years. The three strategies are extreme prices, trend following, and support and resistance. I chose these three strategies because they are well supported by the evidence and offer good prospects for profitable trading in securities.

PART ONE –
BACKGROUND

Chapter One –
The Behavioural Finance Revolution

"There is nothing so dangerous as the pursuit of a rational investment policy in an irrational world."

John Maynard Keynes

What this chapter is about

This chapter shows why behavioural finance is important. Classical economics, on which most of our investment knowledge is based, relied on the concept of rational economic man: a calculating, unemotional participant with a perfect understanding of things around him. Behavioural finance challenged this assumption and broke the classical model, developing new, practical ideas that were more realistic.

This chapter introduces six categories which facilitate our approach to behavioural finance, each the subject of a subsequent chapter, and deals briefly with how behavioural finance can be combined with other investment disciplines.

Why is behavioural finance important for your investments?

Investment is a decision-making process based on the analysis of data and a judgement on risk and uncertainty. Our human nature – be it our emotional side, our brain, or even our physiology – plays an important part in this decision-making process. Behavioural finance studies how people make financial decisions and the strength and weaknesses their human nature brings to the table. Behavioural finance, therefore, lies at the centre of the investment process and it has provided investors with new insights into how to invest their money.

The way we look at financial decisions today is very different from how we looked at them even as little as ten years ago. Behavioural finance has taken the old theories of economics and finance and re-examined them in the light of what psychology and other studies of human behaviour have taught us about the way human beings *actually* act and react – and not how they are supposed to act and react. Most of the pioneers of behavioural finance, therefore, were psychologists and behavioural scientists who applied their knowledge to human beings as economic agents and investors.

One important assumption made by classical economists was that human beings were entirely rational in their economic behaviour. It was assumed that humans analysed everything in a dispassionate and logical manner and only transacted when it was in their interest. Not only this, but it was also assumed that these cold calculations took place against a background of perfect information and, furthermore, were made in such a manner as to optimise the benefit derived by whoever was making the transaction.

Most of classical economics, therefore, was based on the concept of the so-called *rational economic man*, or REM. The subjects of finance and investment are but specialisations of economics and it is therefore no wonder that financial researchers first built upon the economic theories that were at hand when they did their work. These early finance theories are often referred to by behavioural finance practitioners as *standard finance*.

The REM

Rational economic man – a calculating, logical, and emotionless being – was the bedrock of many economic models which were built in the early years of economics.

Suppose the REM wants to buy a car. He might go about it in various ways but is likely to go something like this. He realises he needs to buy the best car for the least costs. He first makes a list of the reasons why he needs a car: to travel to work, go to the cinema, go to the big shopping malls in the suburbs, etc. He then calculates the benefits he is likely to derive from having his own car rather than using public transport, hiring a car on a need basis, calling a taxi, or asking for a lift. Once he has calculated the monetary value of the benefit he is likely to derive, he then goes about looking at the costs.

He realises he needs to collect information about the different cars on offer and he makes a list of all the car vendors in the world. He examines this list and decides that the costs of going to another continent to buy a car are likely to prove prohibitive. He then decides on an appropriate radius in which procurement can reasonably take place. He collects information on all the cars: prices, delivery times, likely maintenance costs, taxes and duties payable, fuel consumption, cost of licences, costs of insurance, etc. He then calculates how long he can use each car for and the disposal value of the car at the end of the period. He then compares the benefits he is likely to derive with the bottom line cost of each model of each make. By the time he makes a decision as to which car to choose he would have worked himself up to be a great expert on cars: he would have near perfect information and his choice is a sharp-pencilled one.

Does REM exist?

Mr REM is really a caricature. Hopefully very few people behave in this obsessive way when they come to buy a car. Mr REM's approach and methods are too time-consuming and, indeed, it is probably a never-ending exercise because by the time Mr REM starts to get somewhere most of his original data is obsolete. If we were to make decisions the REM way, we would probably never arrive at any conclusion.

Yet, we know that there is some truth in my description of the REM. When buying a new car we ask ourselves whether we really need one, or whether we can go by public transport, especially if we live in a big city. We also want to know how much the car would cost us, about fuel efficiency, where best to get the car from and where are we likely to service it. The REM hypothetical model, therefore, is not accurate, but does contain some truth. It does mirror, in certain ways, the way we behave.

In the case under consideration, that of buying a car, we as normal human beings are likely to do two things differently from Mr REM. First, we are unlikely to do as much research, analysis and calculation as Mr REM did. We are likely to keep things much simpler, making fewer mental calculations and comparisons. Otherwise things would get too complex.

Second, we are likely to look at various emotional factors associated with the car. The brand, top speed, the shape of the model, the colours available, and the cachet associated with the vehicle may be important factors to many drivers. To many, a motor car is not simply a machine, but is often nearly a living thing. A car then is more than the sum of its parts and its function is much more than simply taking people and things from point A to point B.

It is no wonder that an economic model which treats cars as simply transportation machines would not reflect all the essential characteristics of the real world and would have, as a consequence, limited utility in describing what is happening and in predicting the future. In a similar fashion, a financial model based on REM does not capture many of the real life and critical aspects of the market it is trying to explain.[1]

The beginnings of behavioural finance

In various ways, the car example brings us to the heart of behavioural finance.

Behavioural finance pioneers realised that while REM was a powerful concept, one that allowed the building of various useful economic theories, it did not capture enough of the truth – it did not capture real human beings with all the emotional baggage and personality humans posses.

We all know that our emotions, such as fear and greed, and the emotions of others, especially if we are part of a crowd, creep surreptitiously into our decision-making and nudge us off the logical path. Often it is only with hindsight that we realise how carried away we actually were. "What was I thinking!" we exclaim when it is too late.

Behavioural finance pioneers felt that economics had to be re-examined and refined placing real, often irrational, often emotional, sometimes capricious, men and women at the centre.

So, behavioural finance can be said to be about the replacement of *homo economicus*, or REM, by *homo sapiens*, real man, in economics. This re-examination of the nature of human beings as economic agents led to important critiques of economic theory by Daniel Kahneman, Amos Tversky, Robert Shiller, Richard Thaler and others, which laid the groundwork for the development of behavioural finance.

---

[1] Please see Appendix 1 for a brief discussion of REM in the market.

Rational within limits

Today, many researchers do not base their work on the superhuman rationality of REM but make use of a more realistic concept, that of *bounded rationality*.

This concept accepts that human beings are essentially rational and given to optimising behaviour but recognises that there are limits to the brain's ability to assimilate and solve complex problems.

> ### Behavioural finance
> Behavioural finance is the application of psychology and other analytical tools to the behaviour of investors.

One aspect of behavioural finance which makes it so fascinating is the study of unexpected, illogical and counter-intuitive decision making. It is precisely this that gives the implications of behavioural finance such importance.

Researchers are now going beyond the study of manifest decisions to explore the human brain in greater depth by means of Magnetic Resonance Imaging (MRI) and other new tools, seeking to understand the very processes whereby an individual arrives at his or her economic decisions. While brain studies continue to elucidate how people make up their minds it is perhaps sobering to note that, ironically, irrational and unpredictable decision-making is likely to always remain the prerogative of human beings. Without uncertainty there would be little scope for learning how to invest.

Investors, for various psychological and physiological reasons, sometimes act illogically, succumb to emotion, make decisions by primitive rules of thumb, have a variable attitude towards risk, sometimes follow the crowd wherever it leads them, let fear or optimism take hold of them, and generally behave in such a way which shows that, after all, markets are all too human. In the next chapter, we shall examine some aspects of the irrationality of humans.

The six categories of behavioural finance

Psychology, unlike some of the other science disciplines, is not built around a unified theory. Instead, it is made up of a large number of theories, hypotheses and experimental results which are not tied together neatly in one grand framework and often seem disparate. Behavioural finance, borrowing so much from psychology, inherited its parent's fragmented nature and this can be somewhat off-putting to investors approaching the subject for the first time.

For this reason, I have classified behavioural finance topics into six main categories. This classification is rather tentative and there are inevitable overlaps but it is the best way I could devise of organising the subject so that an investor taking up this book can form a broad idea of what the main concerns of behavioural finance are. In this way, in his or her further reading, especially when perusing academic papers and the more technical books, the reader will have a rough-and-ready framework on which to hang the different observations and theories.

There may be topics which fall between the six stools, so to speak, and, indeed, as behavioural finance develops, and its ken widens, there may be need for more (or fewer) categories.

The categories

The six main categories are, in turn, divided in two.

First, there are the three categories which deal with our interactions with the world around us:

1. Complexity: coping and dealing with the complexity around us;
2. Perception: the role of perception and how it affects our behaviour;
3. Aversion: our attempt to avoid emotional instability.

Second, there are the three categories dealing with who we are and the influences of those around us:

4. Self: the influence of the self, including status quo;
5. Society: the crowd of which we form part;
6. Gender: behavioural patterns resulting from gender differences.

I call this the CPA-SSG Framework.

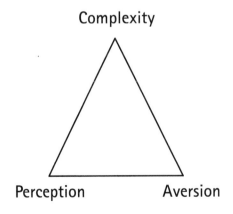

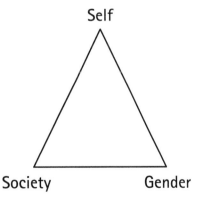

Aversion is a very powerful concept in behavioural finance and fuses together various observations and important studies, including the work on prospect theory. For this reason, this book deals with aversion *after* it deals with the forces of the self. The chapters dealing with each category are therefore as follows:

The six categories of behavioural finance

1. Coping and dealing with complexity: Chapter Three

2. The role of perception: Chapter Four

3. Aversion: Chapter Six

4. The self: Chapter Five

5. The crowd: Chapter Seven

6. Gender issues: Chapter Eight

After looking at how emotions creep into our decision-making in Chapter Two, we look at the first category (Chapter Three), which groups together studies examining how human beings cope and deal with *complexity*. The world we live in is a complex place and the human brain has huge, but still limited, capabilities. Faced with the difficulties which the world – and the marketplace – present, the brain does what it can. It therefore tries to simplify, uses rules of thumb, thinks and observes selectively, looks for patterns and creates its own blind spots.

One fascinating way in which the brain tries to cope is by focusing on changes rather than stationary states. As we shall see, the fact that our brain is better at seeing changes rather than constant states places a limit on our rationality – we normally place more importance on what we gain or lose rather than on what we have.

My second category (Chapter Four) deals with the role of *perception* in behavioural finance. As any painter would tell you, we do not see what is there but what *we think* is there. Indeed, the most difficult part of becoming a realist painter is learning to see what is actually there – not what is *usually* there, not what *photographs* say is there and not what one *supposes* to be there.

The same is true in most academic training: one is learning how to research, how to measure properly, how to be logical, how to detect and remove subjectivity. The human brain has a tendency to see what it wants to see, bands people and events together in a rough-and-ready manner by prototype, gives undue importance to the most recent events rather than the truly important events, comes to conclusions based on hindsight and values data depending on how it is framed. Accountants knew this all along. This is the reason why accounting standards place such a lot of importance on how data is classified, how information is presented and what is material or not.

The third category (Chapter Six) groups behaviour which is driven by *aversion*. We need stability and to "know where we stand". As a general rule, humans do not want frequent change – stability is desirable. Financially, for example, we try to avoid having frequent changes in the value of our portfolio. Up 25% one day and down 20% the following day spells too much adrenalin in too short a time. That's the general rule, though, since sometimes we actively go out and seek adventure, and take a punt on life.

The self is the subject of the fourth category (Chapter Five). What we see and what we do depends on who we are. We may be naturally pessimistic, optimistic, conservative, self-critical, or even given to magical thinking: all of these affect the way we perceive the world, and the way we behave.

For example, if an individual is overconfident, the way they see the market and the way they transact will show this. This is one reason why many investors exclaim that their luck turns bad when they stop paper trading and start the real thing. When paper trading and using notional money investors have less emotional involvement than when using real money. They are less anxious and perhaps more logical. Once they start using real money, they become hesitant, emotional rather than logical, and their trading suffers. This is the main reason why one should start real trading on a small scale. A good deal of becoming a successful trader involves training oneself to gain poise, to act dispassionately in a detached manner and to avoid getting emotionally involved.

We are nearly always part of *the crowd*, part of society. The fifth category, therefore, which is dealt with in Chapter Seven, seeks to draw together how society influences the way we think and the way we feel. As time goes on, more evidence is emerging that our linkages to those around us are wired into our brain. We often observe how people who live for a long time together start to think and speak in similar ways; some say they start to look the same as well.

Chapter Seven also examines how society's feelings and beliefs feed upon themselves and often spiral out of control. These beliefs are often, of course, backed by money and therefore have an influence on markets. As investors, we should be aware of these beliefs and expectations which have taken hold of a market and seek to profit from them, either by going long as a movement starts to develop or by going short when we think it is past its peak. We often observe that once a movement starts, it tends to last longer than many people expect.

At the end of Part Two the sixth category deals with *gender* issues (Chapter Eight). Classical economics and finance did not consider the gender of the persons making investment decisions but behavioural finance shows that gender is a critical variable because men and women have different attitudes towards investing. Men, for example, tend to be overconfident while women are generally conservative. This is a very wide area of research, and work has just begun, but it is likely that investor profiling, especially gender, will become a major issue in future. Gender differences highlight the usefulness of technical analysis in providing a more objective approach to investing.

In Part Three we focus more on how behavioural finance can be combined with technical analysis and quantitative finance to forge a new approach to the market. In Chapter Nine a conceptual framework for understanding three tools of technical analysis – extreme prices, trends, and support and resistance – is introduced and the relevant behavioural finance concepts behind each part of this framework are discussed. Chapter Ten, the final chapter, looks briefly at the new horizons which are opening up and how readers can best put this book to practical use.

The fourth approach

For a long time, writers on investments have spoken of two main approaches to investing.

First, there is the fundamental approach. A security – be it a share in a company or bonds issued by the state – is analysed in terms of its economic characteristics and value. If we are analysing a share in a company, for example, we would ask questions such as:

- What are the profits of the company after tax?

- How many shares does this company have in issue?

- What are the profits as a percentage of turnover?

- Are turnover and profits increasing, stable or declining? Why?

- What is the edge of the company in the market?

- What is the market share of the company?

- What are the strengths, weaknesses, opportunities of the company and what threats does it face (so-called SWOT analysis)?

- What debt level does the company have and is this level sustainable?

- What dividend does the company distribute?

Questions such as these help us gain an understanding of the company, and its likely future cash flows, and thus we can arrive at an idea of its value.

The second approach is technical analysis. In technical analysis, it is primarily the price of the share that is examined, often in the context of the market. Analysts look at how the price of the share changed over time and whether the volume of shares transacted was supportive of the trend in price. Specific patterns are considered, for example the head and shoulders formation, as indicative of a change in trend and others – such as flags – are taken to indicate a continuation of the trend. Simple and moving averages, and the difference between moving averages of different time periods, are also used. It is assumed that by studying price and volume patterns it is possible to predict how the price will change.

Eventually, a third approach, or analytical dimension, emerged; quantitative analysis. Economists took a more universal look at the market and in their new models included all the assets in the world and assumed that participants in this market had good information on which to make decisions. They applied various statistical and mathematical tools to these models of the capital market. The quantitative approach gained prominence in the late 1970s and with it came the various influential models we have today, including the capital asset pricing model and the various models used to value options. New tools were developed as mathematics and statistics were more frequently applied to models of the market, as economists analysed the market to gather evidence to confirm or refute hypotheses and as new quantitative techniques, such as GARCH and fractal geometry, evolved.

Some writers include quantitative finance with the fundamental approach but many writers on technical analysis contend that quantitative finance is actually just a development of their work on price movements and markets. Whatever the classification considerations involved, none of the three approaches really placed the individual investor's psychology at the very centre of its considerations. The individual investor was obviously there but he or she was generally assumed to be behaving as expected; that is rationally. It was behavioural finance which made investors' psychology and behaviour the focus of its studies. In this sense, therefore, behavioural finance can be seen as the much needed fourth approach to investment.

Key concepts in this chapter

- Rational economic man – too ideal a construct
- Bounded rationality – a better model
- The six categories of behavioural finance, the CPA-SSG Framework:
  - Dealing with Complexity
  - Problems of Perception
  - Aversion of instability
  - The Self
  - Society
  - Gender
- Investing:
  - Fundamental approach
  - Technical analysis
  - Analytical/quantitative approach
  - The fourth dimension – behavioural finance

Chapter Two –
People Acting Strange:
Emotion In Decision Making

"My radical version of fallibility is not only an abstract theory but also a personal statement. As a fund manager, I depended a great deal on my emotions. That was because I was aware of the inadequacy of knowledge."

George Soros

What this chapter is about

The reason why we study behavioural finance is because people do not always act rationally – they often do the unexpected. Even when we are on guard for them, emotions still manage to play an important part in decision making. Indeed, without emotions, decisions often become difficult, if not impossible, as we shall see in the case of Buridan's donkey.

This chapter introduces the concepts of heuristics, the rules-of-thumb we often use to make decisions. We also take a look at our behavioural biases, which can be either cognitive or emotional. We will also look briefly at the brain; the hardware where all this is taking place.

The unexpected

At the root of behavioural finance is the fact that people do not always act in a logical manner, as one might expect them to. They sometimes do the unexpected, either wilfully, inadvertently or out of habit.

We see things and situations differently and act in our own way. How and why people act the way they do is the subject of countless tomes. Humanity expends a great intellectual effort in analysing itself.

The strangeness of people's behaviour is what initially drew Professor Daniel Kahneman, as a boy, to the study of psychology. Kahneman, a Nobel Laureate, eventually became one of the pioneers of behavioural finance. In the autobiographical piece which accompanies his acceptance speech for the 2002 Nobel Prize in Economic Sciences he described one experience he remembered vividly. As a Jewish boy living in Nazi-occupied Paris in the 1940s he was subject to a 6pm curfew. One evening he stayed out too late, and on returning home he saw a German soldier approaching. The soldier beckoned him over, hugged him, and showed him a photograph he kept in his wallet, before giving him a gift of some money. Kahneman took this as evidence that people are "endlessly complicated and interesting," and he was attracted to the study of human behaviour by this incident.

This fascination with people and their stories, "touched by irony, and they all had two sides or more" as Kahneman describes them, is what launched him on his great career as one of the pioneers of behavioural finance.

What makes people irrational?

Many of us fancy ourselves to be rational creatures. We believe that we decide on the facts as they are in a logical manner and are careful not to give in to our emotions. The behavioural finance attack on classical economics and its central tenet of rational economic man, while sounding reasonable, seems to us to be something of an affront to this perception of ourselves.

Maybe we do not list all the figures down neatly on a nice sheet of paper and cross every 't', but we believe we have all of our emotions under control and only let them interfere, if at all, when we want to, that is.

It is not quite so. We often do not even realise that our emotions have crept into the equation. At other times, what we think we are seeing is different from what actually exists. We tint facts and figures with our emotional sunglasses and arrive at non-rational conclusions.

Biases and heuristics

Human decision-making is fraught with irrationality. Indeed, most of behavioural finance is concerned with the study of this irrationality.

By irrational we signify a departure from the strictly objective and logical even though, ultimately, benefit may be derived from such irrationality. I am sure, for example, that when most people lend money to a friend or donate money to charity, they derive a psychological benefit from doing so.

Irrationality stems from two sources: biases and heuristics. In turn, there are two kinds of biases: cognitive and emotional.

Figure 2.1: Source of irrationality

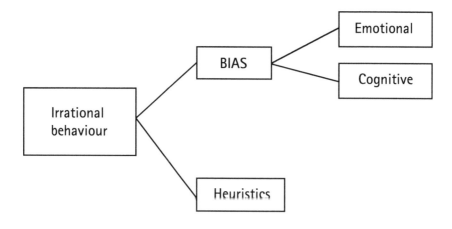

Biases

A bias is a systematic error in the way we process information about the world around us. A bias can be contrasted to a random error. While a bias involves making an error consistently whenever the same set of circumstances exist, a random error does not manifest itself in a consistent manner, even though the circumstances might be identical.

We sometimes suffer from biases because of the way we perceive the world around us, because of our *cognition*. The investigation of cognitive biases seems to have dominated research, perhaps because they are easier to understand and easier to delineate than emotional biases, and they are more susceptible to experimentation. At other times, we suffer (or sometimes even benefit) from certain biases, and act irrationally, because we let our *emotions* interfere or are unable to keep them from interfering. We may not even realise that emotions are playing a role. How emotions infiltrate our decision-making is the subject of this chapter.

Appendix 2 gives a list of biases and classifies them into the two categories.

Heuristics

Another reason why we sometimes seem to be acting irrationally is because, faced with the complexity of the environment around us, we often make use of rough-and-ready rules of thumb, or heuristics (see box). Heuristics simplify our environment, making our lives easier, but they can often lead us astray.

Heuristic

Heuristic (pronounced hyoo-ris-tik) comes from the Greek *heuriskein* meaning to find out and discover.

In behavioural finance heuristics refers to the rules of thumb used to make decisions, and the errors associated with their use, in contrast to the dictionary meaning of heuristics as being the processes and techniques by means of which people learn, discover and solve problems often via experimentation, improvisation and trial-and-error methods.

The heuristic process involves guesswork and trial and error rather than an algorithm or a structured formula. Heuristics are expedient and have the benefit of speed.

How does emotion come into it?

Behavioural finance studies the role of human emotion in investment decision making.

If you think that you can sanitise your financial decisions from all emotion, this simple experiment should come as a rude shock:

> I have two boxes in front of me. One contains a certain number of gold coins and the other contains double that number of gold coins. You are invited to pick one of the boxes and to look inside it. You then have the choice of either accepting that box or rejecting it and opening the other one. If you opt for the second box, you cannot then go back to the first box.

You have now looked inside the first box. It has ten shiny gold coins. Would you like to stay put or go to the second one?

Two main emotions can be said to be at play here. If I stay with the first box, maybe the second box contains twenty coins. Human beings are by nature optimists and they want more and therefore the expectation, the hope, is that there is more on the other side, that the other side is greener. On the other hand, you know that if you went for the second box and found five coins, you would have lost five coins, and regret it.

These two emotions, hope and greed versus regret and fear, are part and parcel of all investment decisions. This is the important point. When you invest, you are attaching uncertainty to your capital today in expectation of gains tomorrow. To invest you have to be by nature an optimist, and to want more, and to be willing to risk incurring the pain of fear and regret.

Figure 2.2: Emotion in investment decisions

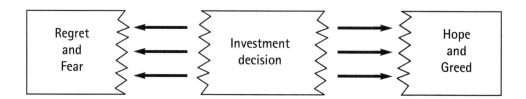

As we shall see, there are many emotions involved in our decisions and they manifest themselves in our behaviour and perceptions. Indeed, can we make decisions if we take out all emotion? This question brings us to one of history's most important donkeys.

Buridan's ass

The idea of rational behaviour assumes that one always does something for a reason, that there is a prior cause for our actions. Otherwise, our behaviour would be simply frivolous rather than rational. It is assumed, for example, that between a beneficial action and an unbeneficial one, a person would choose the beneficial one. Between two beneficial actions, a person would choose the more beneficial of the two.

John Buridan came to study this aspect of human behaviour because, in the first half of the 14th century, he was at the forefront of a movement which was trying to extract secular philosophy from theology. He had a new vision of philosophy as a pursuit based on what is evident to the senses, and what is logical to the human mind, rather than one based on the truths as revealed in scripture and doctrine.

The donkey's problem, which we shall now look into, had been contemplated before Buridan. Indeed, there are versions of it going back to Aristotle. But since Buridan must have written about it, or discussed it, the donkey's problem has been handed down to us as the case of *Buridan's ass*.

It goes like this:

> Suppose it is high noon and you have a very thirsty donkey standing in the middle of a yard. Five feet to his left there is a bucket filled to the brim with water. Five feet to his right, at precisely the same angle, there is an identical bucket also filled to the brim with water. The donkey, of course, needs to drink badly but to which bucket shall it go? To the one on the right or to the one on the left?

This is the paradox of Buridan's ass. As the paradox would have it, if the donkey is logical, acting only on prior cause, it will just stand there looking at the buckets full of water and die of thirst. There is no reason at all for it to choose one bucket over the other. The donkey would defer its decision to the point of suicide. If the donkey is not rational, if it is mad, then it might avoid suicide by making an arbitrary decision.

Theoretically, if one has to decide between two identical situations, and there is no emotion involved, there is no basis for a decision and a decision might never be made. Buridan's ass is a neat armchair experiment which throws some interesting light on the central role of emotion in decision making.

Brain damage

Buridan and his donkey pose an interesting question: would someone who has suffered brain damage and lost the faculties of emotion be able to make decisions?

The prefrontal cortex, the front of the brain, deals with the thought processes, emotions and memories concerned with judgement and can thus be described as the operations centre for decision making. Antonio Damasio, a neuroscientist, studied people with injuries to their prefrontal cortex. These people seemed normal in all respects other than that they had lost their appreciation of emotion. Damasio reported that the ability of these people to make decisions was seriously impaired. They could describe all the factors surrounding a particular decision, and would know what the outcomes would be for different actions, but could not choose between alternative courses of action because it was not clear to them whether they preferred a 'good' or 'bad' outcome. Uncannily, Damasio's findings seem to support Buridan's thought experiments.

The sneaky subconscious

The links between memory, emotion and decision making first started coming to light early in the 20th century. Eduard Claparede, a Swiss doctor, noticed that amnesiac patients who seemed to have lost all their memory – who had to be reminded of who the people around them were every 15 minutes – somehow managed to remember certain things unconsciously. In a classic experiment, Claparede first concealed a small pin in his hand and then welcomed a lady suffering from severe amnesia by shaking her hand. Next time they met, she was reluctant to shake hands with Claparede. When asked, the lady did not know why she hesitated.

This fascinating field of research continues to develop and new techniques in brain imaging have given it a boost. More and more light is being constantly thrown on what brain activity is involved in decision making. This bodes well for exciting developments in behavioural finance.

At University College, London, for example, Benedetto De Martino and his colleagues ran brain scans on 20 men and women whilst they were gambling, in order to study, in particular, how *framing* affected decisions. The subjects were given a choice whether to gamble or not. Gambling decisions, averaging two seconds in duration, fired up the part of the brain called the amygdala, an almond-shaped region at the centre of the brain, slightly forward of the ear axis.

The amygdala is concerned with the primary negative emotions, such as fear, and retains memories of an emotional nature. The amygdala prepares us for the fight or flight response during sudden emergencies. Someone whose amygdala has been damaged would be able to remember the details of an event but not the associated emotions.

Activity was also reported in the prefrontal cortex, corroborating Damasio's work about the important role of the prefrontal cortex in decision making. The prefrontal cortex came into action when subjects were thinking over the two choices presented to them, in this case to gamble or not to gamble.

De Martino and his colleagues also found that activity in the anterior cingulate cortex (ACC) evidences conflict between analytical and emotional responses. This part of the cortex lies in the front, top middle of the brain and seems to occupy a strategic area since it forms the front part of a 'collar' around the corpus callosum, which is the nerve bundle that relays neural signals between the right and left cerebral hemispheres of the brain. The ACC appears to have both autonomic functions – such as regulating the heart rate and blood pressure – as well as rational cognitive functions, such as reward anticipation, decision making and various emotions including empathy. It seems that damage to it leads to reduced levels of tension and anger.

The attraction of money

Studies have shown that the expectation of monetary rewards trigger the same brain activity as good tastes, pleasant music, addictive drugs and sex.

The nucleus accumbens lies above the amygdala and is responsible for reward, motivation and addiction. Certain drugs, like cocaine and nicotine, lead to the release of dopamine. Dopamine is a chemical associated with the neural pleasure system and is released in reaction to, or in anticipation of, a pleasurable stimulus. Once released, it goads people on. It seems to either flood the neural system or abandon it, leading to alternative states of high pleasure or depression. Investors who have plunged from the high of watching profits accumulate to the low of mounting losses understand the effects of dopamine perfectly.

How the different functional aspects of the brain come together, how dopamine and other chemicals (such as serotonin, noradrenaline, and testosterone) interact with the brain and the nervous system, and which part of the brain does what, is a hugely complex area of research. Brain research is one of the ultimate frontiers of science and new findings are being published constantly.

Sleep

If you are suffering from lack of sleep, **do not trade**.

Under conditions of sleep deprivation, the nucleus accumbens becomes more active when high risk-high payoff choices were made. At the same time, the brain's response to losses are dampened.

Lack of sleep elevates the expectation of gains and makes light of one's losses following risky decisions.

(Based on the study by Vinod Venkatraman and colleagues at Duke University.)

These observations on emotions in decision making seem to suggest that our decision making is the result of the dynamic interaction between our rational and emotional sides. An interesting paper in this regard is 'Risk as Analysis and Risk as Feelings,' in which the authors note that:

> "People base their judgements of an activity or a technology not only on what they think about it but also on what they feel about it. If they like an activity, they are moved toward judging the risks as low and the benefits as high; if they dislike it, they tend to judge the opposite – high risk and low benefit. Under this model, affect comes prior to, and directs, judgements of risk and benefit."

Rationality versus emotion

We know, therefore, that human beings make financial decisions in a "dance of affect and reason," as Slovic et al, the writers of the 'Risk as Analysis' paper put it. While business culture seems to abhor emotional decision making, we know that emotion pokes its nose into our financial considerations, often without our being conscious of it, simply because we are wired that way.

Many writers and researchers recommend that we should use this knowledge about how our brain functions during decision making to control our emotions, try to figure out where they are leading us and sanitise our mental processes. While this is easier said than done, recent developments seem to support rationality versus emotion. A study has shown, for example, that people with brain damage that impaired their emotions outperformed other people in an investment game since they were more willing to take high-payoff risks and were less likely to react to losses. They finished the game with 13% more money.

One of the co-authors of this study on brain damage and risk, Antoine Bechara, noted that "It's possible that people who are high risk-takers or good investors may have what you call a functional psychopathy. They don't react emotionally to things. Good investors can learn to control their emotions in certain ways to become like those people." On the other hand, we must be aware that those same emotions which we consider to be a hindrance to our logic are also a survival mechanism – emotionless risk-taking can lead to taking on excessive risks. In real life, the emotions associated with our financial decisions often come in useful by limiting our losses. It seems that the best traders are those who manage to detach themselves from daily profits and losses and look at their investments statistically.

As Ed Seykota put it:

"Risk is a combination of the possibility of a loss and the magnitude of the loss. We register risk in our bodies as a feeling of fear. One way to manage various forms of risk, including prospective risk, initial risk, open risk, and unconscious risk is to make sure your feeling of fear is an ally, fully functioning on your emotional instrument panel. In our medicinal culture, some people attempt to mediate fear, rather than manage risk. In general, people with willingness to experience fear and other feelings are better risk managers than those who have fear in knots or fear under the influence of narcotics."

Key concepts covered in this chapter

- Heuristics
- Biases:
  - Cognitive
  - Emotional
- Buridan's donkey
- The brain:
  - Prefrontal cortex
  - Amygdala
- Sleep deprivation
- Risk and fear

PART TWO –

BEHAVIOURAL FINANCE

Chapter Three –
Complexity: Trying To Keep Things Simple

"I soon learned to scent out what was able to lead to fundamentals and to turn aside from everything else, from the multitude of things that clutter up the mind."

Albert Einstein

What this chapter is about

We try to cope with the complexity around us using simplification, filtering, isolation and withdrawal. This chapter deals with each of these in turn.

We often simplify by the use of heuristics. We filter by sorting data and by focusing on what is changing. There are various forms of withdrawal: some are direct, like rejection and wishful thinking; others are indirect, such as when we seek confirmation and when we perceive selectively. The way we deal with complexity often determines our decisions.

The main reason why behavioural finance studies complexity is because financial markets are complex and we often observe, unsurprisingly, that the way investors cope with complexity in financial markets has many parallels to the how people try and deal with the complex environments in which they live.

Trying to keep it simple

I am a true believer in simplicity but, try as I might, I always find complexity creeping in around me. I have discussed this with various friends of mine. Some say they never think about such things and take things in life as they come. Some say they do not try to keep things simple because it is no use, and yet others say they are in much the same quandary as I am.

Simplicity has various advantages:

- It makes it possible for us to understand things without much effort.

- It makes things easy to remember.

- It is difficult for us to get lost in simplicity.

- Simple tasks and concepts can be more easily evaluated.

- Simplicity liberates our minds to do other things.

- It aids communication.

- It saves time.

Complexity has the opposite effects.

Generally, simple is easy, complex is hard. And yet, complex things are made of simple things. The underlying structure of many things which appear to us to be complex is actually quite simple. But when we focus on this simple underlying structure, we again find great complexity. I call this the simple-complex paradox.

Tax laws

In my lectures I like to use the example of tax laws. The tax laws of any major country are complex. One can argue that many are unnecessarily complex but at least there is a case to be made for their complexity: tax laws are trying to raise money from a complex world made up of reluctant payers, but to do so with some degree of fairness. The degree of fairness with which they do this varies from country to country but in the UK, for example, where a lot of effort and attention is given to trying to be fair, the tax laws are riddled with provisions, exceptions and counter-exceptions making the whole set of tax laws incredibly complex.

However, if one just picks one random section of the tax code and reads it, one finds that the concepts involved are usually rather simple. The section itself, taken on its own, seems rather straightforward. The complexity then multiplies rapidly when one goes up (looking at other sections which take meaning from that section), when one goes sideways (studying other sections which somehow refer to that section), or downwards (into the meaning of the individual words or phrases used). What the words mean usually opens such a can of worms that serious problems end up before the courts, who go to extraordinary lengths of logic to try and explain them.

Even if we try and keep things simple, even if the underlying structure of all that which is around us is simple, complexity creeps in. In fact, over time, there is a drift towards complexity as well as specialisation and diversity.

Financial complexity

Finance starts with a very simple concept: what you have (the assets) are either borrowed (liabilities) or owned outright (equity). One then heads towards complexity by considering debit and credit to the respective three types of account. Complexity gears up by having many individuals and enterprises interacting together each for his, her or its own purposes. Financial complexity reaches its epitome when you allow third parties to participate in all of this, and in what the future might hold, by means of the capital markets including derivatives and various forms of insurance.

Coping with complexity

Humans have always had to cope with complexity in order to survive. Indeed, over the ages, man has managed not only to cope with complexity, but to deal with it rather well, and sometimes even to use it for his own advantage.

The first thing the brain tries to do, when faced with complexity, is to try and simplify it. Simplification is an important tool when dealing with complexity. As we shall see, simplification involves the use of heuristics, stereotypes and conjunction: helpful, but often misleading, techniques.

When faced with complexity, we also try to filter out the noise and concentrate on what is important. When we visit a fair, there are many things going all around us but we try to concentrate on the activities that interest us. Another thing we do is to ignore similarities between alternative proposals. This is called the isolation effect. If we are looking around for a bicycle, we don't pay too much attention to the two wheels, since all bicycles have two wheels. Rather we tend to look at distinguishing features, such as weight, colour, gears and the type of light used.

If nothing helps, we withdraw, and bury our heads in the sand. We pray that we don't see and are not seen. Behaviour under withdrawal is not as simple as we might expect it to be. We shall briefly examine various forms which withdrawal can take because withdrawal, too, is very relevant to financial decision making.

Dealing with complexity:

- Simplification •   Filtering

- Isolation •   Withdrawal

Simplifying by heuristic

In Chapter Two we saw that human beings sometimes appear irrational because they make use of heuristics. Heuristics, as you recall, are rules of thumb we use to simplify our decision making.

People look around them at what is happening and form an opinion in their mind of the forces at work and the behaviour of things. From the patterns they see, they come up with a heuristic to both describe what is happening and with which they hope to predict the future. But heuristics are necessarily a crude model of reality. They contain errors and they may lead us into more errors.

The trend is one of the most often used heuristics in financial markets. We assume that if something has happened and continues to happen then it is likely to continue happening for some time. The trend heuristic has been observed in a number of studies. Werner De Bondt did very interesting work on this topic and he calls this behaviour "betting on trends." In one of his many papers, De Bondt describes some very interesting evidence from a survey he conducted of individual investors. He found that their stock price forecasts were anchored in past performance, investors showed excessive optimism, were overconfident and underestimated the degree to which stocks moved in tandem with the market (the beta).

Trends are re-visited in Chapter Nine once other concepts in behavioural finance have been introduced.

People tend to simplify not only by the use of rules of thumb but also by classifying what they see around them into categories. In an attempt to put complexity in some sort of order, people tend to try and find representatives, or create stereotypes. This is called *representativeness* and this behaviour creates big problems in finance, as it sometimes does in real life. We shall deal with representativeness in Chapter Four.

Filtering out the noise

The environment around us continually bombards us with data. Data is not important in itself but is the basic building block for information. Information is data which has been processed by our brain to become useful for our thinking and understanding. From the multitude of data which hits us every minute of the day, we have to decide what is important and what is not, what ought to be processed and what should be ignored. Data has to be filtered and, even when some of the data is processed into information, that information itself should be filtered further. Information then becomes knowledge and understanding and, with time, hopefully, wisdom.

Filtering simplifies our life and requires a much smaller brain than we would need if we were to process all the data which we see, hear, taste, touch or smell. At higher levels, filtering usually enhances our understanding by letting us focus on information and concepts which are valid and which carry knowledge forwards. I say *usually* because sometimes filtering leads to ignoring vital facts or information. While filtering is generally positive, we have to be careful to evaluate and re-evaluate data and information as we go along. This is as true in investing as in any other field of intellectual endeavour.

The quote from Albert Einstein at the opening of this chapter deals with avoiding noise; "the multitude of things that clutter up the mind." Noise is data or even information which we consider to be without meaning and which we want to discard.

Focusing on movement

A very important way our brain distinguishes between data and noise and hitting upon what to process further is differentiating between change and a maintained state.

A maintained state is when things stay pretty much as they are. Change, of course, is when the state of things changes.

First, an example from ordinary life. You are driving on a road where the speed limit is 60mph. You are driving in the slow lane and there are other cars around you moving at the same speed. You see these cars as either stationary or moving slowly forward or falling slowly back. All of a sudden, from nowhere, a red car drives past you in the fast lane at speed. Your eyes lock on it temporarily for you to determine what is going to happen. The car continues quickly on its way. After a while, you cannot see it any more and you forget about it. Again, your brain settles down and you are just observing passively, keeping your eyes open but not focusing on anything in particular. Then, the guy in front of you swerves into the fast lane. Again, you pay attention, to see what is happening. Or you notice that the truck behind you is coming up too close for comfort.

You get the idea. Anything which changes attracts our attention. Anything which does not change, or does not change much, so called maintained states, we do not waste too much mental energy on. This mechanism is crucial for our survival. Merchants knew about all this long ago, of course. It is one reason why displays in shop windows are rearranged periodically.

Financial information

Change versus maintained state is very important when one is investing money.

The data raining down on an investor is tremendous. There is the printed media, finance TV channels and the internet, all being fed by corporations (to promote what they sell and to provide information to shareholders), governments, central banks, academics, news agencies, educators, commentators, securities exchanges, other investors, gossipers and more. Analyses of the basic information builds up the layers. Again, the writers and producers of this information have a particular viewpoint to put across. The nature of the source has to be kept in perspective. The investor has to balance two needs: the need to be informed and the need to avoid overload and stay sane. The investor must therefore filter the information available.

I try to focus my systems on capturing change. I want to detect, analyse and understand the changes that are occurring. Which currencies moved appreciably over different time horizons? Which stock, commodities, and other assets are moving? Where are the blips in economic statistics? By detecting and studying the changes that are occurring I would know what is happening and how things are moving, and how and which trends are forming.

Isolation

One good way to cope with complexity is to just look at what is different. Earlier, we noted how someone buying a bicycle focuses their attention on the features which distinguish one bicycle from another. In a similar way, an investment analyst studying soybean producers does not focus on the trifoliate leaves of the soybean plant but on how the different producers operate, the likely effects of the weather, transportation issues, the fertilisers used, etc. He would pay attention to the common factors, such as the leaves, only if a particular farm has a special weakness or strength in that regard – for example, a ravenous endogenous insect. This focus on what is different preserves our mental energy for that which is normally important.[2]

In a way, this mechanism is parallel to the 'what's moving?' mechanism – here, too, human beings focus on what is different and, by implication, what is most important.

Withdrawal

Rejection

The most obvious form of withdrawal is rejection. In rejection a person facing complexity, often accompanied by losses or other adverse events, simply refuses reality and shuts down contact with his or her environment.

A vivid case is that of Grinning Gilbert, narrated by Barton Biggs in his book *Hedgehogging*. In the mid-1990s, Grinning Gilbert had left his job as portfolio manager with an established firm and set up a successful hedge fund. Eventually he moved to Greenwich, Connecticut, and played up his role by buying a big stone mansion, a huge wine cellar and recruiting three technical analysts. The overhead he was carrying was huge, especially since the family was continually splurging money, encouraged by the internet boom. The market turned, however, and for the year 2000 his fund was down 15% and many partners in his hedge fund were feeling queasy. By mid-2001 he was down another 30%. Then, as Biggs relates, "One Tuesday, in early October, after a morning when his longs were down and his shorts were up and after several limited partners screamed at him," Grinning Gilbert went home and locked himself up in his bedroom, eating toast and soup, and did not come out until his wife closed down the fund. They then put the house up for sale and moved to San Diego.

This is an extreme reaction but illustrates the case superbly. Often, of course, rejection of bad news is not so absolute as to bring about a total shutdown. We usually simply shut our mind to the bad news and the consequences.

---

[2] I say normally, of course, because sometimes what we take for granted as being no different actually is and becomes the most important factor we need consider.

We buy a security and we think it is going to continue going up, but it turns and starts falling. We look at the first small loss and we put it down to normal market fluctuation. The loss gets bigger and we believe it's just a bad patch, soon to be over. Other securities continue to perform well so we then start seriously suspecting that something is wrong with the security we are in. Then, as usually happens, the bad news surfaces when we are carrying this huge loss.

We start hoping against hope that there would be a turnaround, that something will happen which will take away the pain from our loss. The loss gets worse. We then put the security in the 'graveyard' portfolio amongst the other wretcheds, the short-term investments which went awry and are now considered to be long-term investments, hoping that some day a phoenix will rise from the ashes. And we forget about the security.

As you would have noticed, rejection of reality often involves a lot of wishful thinking. As investors, we have to watch out for this. While all wise investment decisions involve contemplating alternative future scenarios, wishful thinking goes beyond this in that it involves imbuing a particular favourable scenario with emotion and, as a result, we start believing that a particular scenario is more likely than it actually is.

Confirmation bias – telling yourself you were right

Perhaps more insidious than rejection is confirmation bias.

Confirmatory bias makes us give more importance to information which supports our beliefs than to information which negates it, or which puts it in doubt. As discussed, when faced with complexity, we have a tendency to see what we think is important for the decision at hand. We therefore tend to resort to selective perception. Selective perception allows us to concentrate on what we think is important but makes us exclude information which we think is not but which, nevertheless, might contribute significantly to our quest for the optimum solution.

Confirmation bias often creeps in without our knowledge. Not only is it easier and more congenial for us to deal with information which confirms our thoughts but we also tend to go beyond the pleasant feeling and give confirmatory information even more importance than it deserves, while giving information which is adverse to our thoughts less importance than we ought to. We therefore emphasise evidence which supports what *we think* rather than basing our ideas upon the evidence. Confirmation bias makes us ask questions that when answered will support our beliefs.

Evidence which does not fit the scheme of things in our mind is either ignored, faulted, or tested against a higher standard – for example, a blurry picture of a UFO is enough for a believer in extraterrestrial life, but an informed opinion that the picture has been doctored needs to be backed by reams of evidence. Confirmation bias, therefore, tends to make our information gathering lopsided and this leads our decision making further astray.

One reason for the confirmation bias is to avoid cognitive dissonance, that is conflict between two or more ideas, for example ideas coming from what we believe and ideas from evidence we come across. Cognitive dissonance causes discomfort and we therefore avoid it.

In investment decision making, we have to guard against confirmation bias. We buy stock in a company and follow the news which it releases. We are delighted with positive news because it confirms our wisdom in acquiring the shares. We tend to consider any bad news which is released as being just a temporary setback. We tend to not give good news published by the company's competitors its due importance.

Seeing things clearly, the good with the bad, is an important skill for the investor. Evidence has to be evaluated objectively; indeed, seeking evidence, examining evidence objectively, and checking whether this evidence falsifies a previously delineated hypothesis lies at the heart of the scientific method.

The Forer Effect

Those of us who still glance at the astrology sections in magazines to get an inkling of what's in store can't help noticing that the way the piece is written is meant precisely for us. You might hear someone say, "That's so me!" This is called the Forer effect.

The Forer effect is an aspect of subjective validation in which words, symbols, and signs are considered to be valid because the person receiving the data or information finds them personally meaningful.

If one read under one's astrological sign that it is a lucky day to invest and imbue this conjecture with meaning, one might go ahead and invest, even though there might be no financial justification.

Barn door closing

Sometimes, when people are overwhelmed with complexity, and their brains cannot process the information, they often just resort to an action which worked in the past. This is referred to as a barn-door-closing solution.

Complexity and investing

Often, in dealing with the complex environment of investing, people not only try and simplify what they perceive but also focus their attention on what they think is important at the time they are making their financial decisions. One of the ways they do this is by focusing on what is changing rather than what remains constant. Another is to isolate the characteristics which they consider unique to that particular situation.

When things go wrong, investors may withdraw by rejecting the validity of news. If prices fall, for example, wishful thinking makes them believe that a reversal will soon take place. They tend to give credence to what confirms their beliefs and see only what they like to see.

While simplification, filtering and isolation usually improves decision making – or, at least, makes for speedier decisions – the decisions taken during withdrawal tend to be imperfect.

Key concepts in this chapter

- Simplification
- Filtering:
    - Data, information, knowledge, understanding, wisdom
    - Change versus the maintained state
- Isolation
- Withdrawal:
    - Rejection
    - Wishful thinking
    - Confirmation bias
    - Selective perception
- Forer effect, subjective validation
- Barn door closing

Chapter Four –
Perception: What You See Is Not Always What You Get

"The farther backward you can look, the farther forward you can see."

Winston Churchill

What this chapter is about

In the previous chapter we saw how our attempts to deal with our complex environment can lead us to some pretty irrational behaviour. This chapter deals with perhaps an even more irksome problem: even if we try our best to understand the complex world around us, our perception works tricks on us.

There are a number of fundamental behavioural finance concepts explored in this chapter. It starts off with cognitive biases, such as hindsight, and proceeds to examine the errors caused by comparisons, the representativeness bias, the conjunction fallacy, the gambler's fallacy, sample-size neglect, the availability heuristic and recency bias. These illustrate how we often erroneously base our decisions on irrelevant features, on assumptions rather than facts, on what we suppose should happen, on what we see most often or what we have seen recently.

We also tend to make decisions based on the way the problem is framed or how we mentally account for it.

This chapter will also look at the process of anchoring and adjustment, how we change our decisions gradually, based on what has gone on before and what we perceive has happened.

Later chapters, particularly Chapter Ten, will use these concepts to explain common price graph patterns.

Cognitive biases

In Chapter Two we saw how human decision making can be seen as being influenced by three kinds of biases and in that chapter the first kind of bias – the emotional bias – was introduced. In Chapter Three we looked at heuristic biases and examined the ways they assist and hinder decision making. In this chapter we are going to take a closer look at the third kind of bias – cognitive bias – and examine how this impacts our decision making.

Cognitive bias is the misperception of reality. We often see things not as they are but as our mind imagines them to be.

Perhaps the clearest and most ubiquitous example of a cognitive bias is hindsight. We all know how smart we are with hindsight. You might hear people say such things as: "It was quite obvious to me that Google was going to be a great success!", "I was going to put all my money in Microsoft stock but my wife did not let me!" and "It is obvious that the main cause of World War II was the Treaty of Versailles." People with heavy doses of hindsight bias not only re-write history but come to believe they are superior thinkers. This makes them underestimate uncertainty and leads to bad decisions.

What is really fascinating about history is that it is written with the benefit of hindsight, but things must have looked uncertain at the time. It is the same with investment. Hindsight works wonders but it works too late, and so investment becomes a matter of probabilities and luck. As investors, we must work hard to get at the facts and to try and figure out the odds. All this work, hopefully, should enable us to tilt the odds in our favour – but there are no guarantees.

Cognitive biases can have various effects on our thinking and behaviour. We shall here examine their effects on decision making, with special reference to finance, but we have to keep in mind that, to human beings, reality is often what we see, not what is out there. As a result, cognitive biases can have serious consequences, not just on financial decisions but also on health.

People suffering from various types of cognitive distortions, for example, fall into negative thinking, get entangled in various negative emotions and eventually suffer from depression and anxiety. Cognitive therapy helps them to restructure their cognition. As human beings, therefore, and as decision makers, we have to be aware of cognitive biases so that we be on guard for them.

Comparisons are noxious

In trying to understand the world around us, we have a natural tendency to compare one thing with another.

In order to understand the performance of a student, I compare her to others in her class. To understand how BP plc is doing, I compare it with Royal Dutch Shell or with Chevron. This enables me to elucidate what the similarities and differences are and allows me to come to an opinion as to performance over that particular class of students or companies. Comparison, therefore, is generally a great tool for us to understand the world around us.

Yet comparisons lead us into many errors. Let us look at some obvious examples.

We often compare one thing with another directly. The price of this TV set was $4000 but is now $3000. To us this looks like a big saving of $1000 but, actually, we realise after a while that the going price for such TV sets is $3000. It seems cheap only by comparison to its previous high price. To reverse the example, if the $3000 was a sale price tag and we find a week later that the price has been jacked up to $3500, we are unlikely to want to buy it and would rather wait.

We also compare what is happening today, or what is about to happen, with what happened in the past. Would you pay $50 for a two litre bottle of water? If you had never previously paid so much for two litres of water, you would be unlikely to accept this price. But what if you were stuck in the middle of the Sahara?

Another group of comparison errors arise from comparing now with the future. You obviously prefer $100 now to $100 in a month's time. But would you prefer $100 now to $110 in a month's time? Most people would, even though the implied interest rate is 10% per month. Various experiments have shown that people apply a huge discount rate to future earnings. It is one reason why many fail to save for retirement and would rather spend the money now.

The representativeness bias

Linda

Linda must be the most famous lady in behavioural finance. She is the subject of an important experiment devised by Tversky and Kahneman, which goes as follows:

> Linda is a 31 year old who is single, outspoken and very bright. She majored in philosophy. As a student she was deeply concerned with issues of discrimination and social justice, and also participated in antinuclear demonstrations.

Which is more likely?

1. Linda works in a bank.

2. Linda works in a bank and is active in the feminist movement.

Did you chose the second answer? If not, you're amongst the minority, who are correct.

Many classify Linda as a feminist, answer (2), because her characteristics, as stated in the question, are similar to those we imagine feminist activists to have.

The representativeness bias makes us classify people or events in a certain class because the characteristics of those people or events seem to match those of that class. Suffering from this bias, therefore, we decide by type rather than classify after an examination of the true facts and the probabilities. We go by stereotype.

Those who chose answer (2) did so because they had classified Linda as a feminist and ignored the probabilities in the case. There are more people working in a bank than people who both work in a bank and are active feminists. Answer (1) is much more probable than answer (2). Yet the representativeness bias, which can also be considered as a representativeness heuristic, leads us to disregard the probabilities and make a decision on characteristics.

Experxample

Behavioural finance literature is replete with clever examples that double up as experiments.

The Linda example is one such. It is an example which serves to elicit answers to show the way we think. Used in questionnaires, such experxamples, as I call them, bring out many of the main principles and findings of behavioural finance.

N.B. Experxamples differ from parables because the latter are examples meant to illustrate a moral or spiritual truth.

Linda's experxample can also be used to illustrate what a **conjunction fallacy** is.

Logically, a general condition is more probable than a specific one. For example, there are more men than men with glasses.[3] In this case, the conjunction fallacy tricks us into thinking that a person with a specific condition (a man with glasses) is more likely than a person with a more general condition (a man), even though the latter is much more abundant.

What type of investment is this?

In finance, even amongst professionals, the representativeness bias is very common.

For example, in order to cope with the complexities which thousands of companies listed on major securities exchanges involve, we often classify the stocks of such companies as being, say, growth stocks, income stocks or value stocks. Each analyst, or each house, gives its own classification but these classifications tend to mask many dissimilarities.

We would tend to assume that if both Company A and Company B are growth stocks, then Company A is very similar to Company B. This is something every investor should watch out for. Even though two companies might both be growth stocks, they might be very different and susceptible to very different influences. One might be a company in solar technology while another might be involved in government logistics and outsourcing. Both are currently growth areas but what influences one company tends to be very different from what influences the other.

We see the same thing happening with hedge funds. If you are running a fund-of-hedge-funds, and you are trying to choose amongst the thousands of hedge funds

---

[3] This logic is also at the basis of Occam's razor which, put simply, states: all things being equal, the simplest hypothesis or solution is usually the best. In my example, if you do not know what type of creature it is, it is more likely to be a man than a man with glasses. Occam's razor is also called the law of parsimony (in latin *lex parsimoniae*) because it goes to the bare bones of the matter – and not because the principle is attributed to William of Ockham, a friar in one of the two Mendicant Orders, the Franciscans (the other mendicant Order being the Dominicans).

available, you have to adopt some sort of classification in order to be able to simplify what exists out there. Once you do this, you can measure the performance of the different classes and, armed with this, you can then proceed to form an idea of the hedge funds you should include in your portfolio.

The Credit Suisse/Tremont Hedge Fund Index, for example, which is the first asset-weighted hedge fund index, classifies hedge funds according to the investment style they adopt. It has adopted a classification system which is orthodox in the industry. See Figure 4.1.

Figure 4.1: Credit Suisse/Tremont classification of hedge fund managers' investment style

Credit Suisse/Tremont Hedge Fund Index

In order to construct the index, Credit Suisse/Tremont classify hedge fund managers' styles into the following ten sub-strategies:

1. Convertible arbitrage:
   Exploiting price inefficiencies between convertible securities and stock.

2. Dedicated short bias:
   Equity and derivatives portfolios with net short, bearish focus.

3. Emerging markets:
   Equity and fixed-income investments in emerging markets worldwide.

4. Equity market-neutral:
   Offsetting long and short equity positions that are beta-neutral, currency-neutral, or both.

5. Event-driven:
   Corporate strategies focused on distressed securities, high-yield debt, Regulation D and risk arbitrage.

6. Fixed-income arbitrage:
   Exploiting price inefficiencies between related debt securities.

7. Global macro:
   Directional macroeconomic strategies.

8. Long-short equity:
   Directional equity and equity derivative strategies.

9. Managed futures:
   Listed futures strategies often driven by technical or market analysis.

10. Multi strategy:
    Multiple strategies.

Source: Credit Suisse/Tremont Hedge Index, www.hedgeindex.com

In spite of this neat, and very useful, classification, hedge fund managers are notorious for what is called style drift. Their style might start off as being long-short equity but, during the course of the year, they discover some new method which they believe will give them a better edge on the market and shift into it, eventually finishing the year with a sizable part of the portfolio under, say, equity market-neutral. This causes huge problems for fund-of-hedge-funds managers and some retain the right to exclude from their portfolios funds which drift away from their original style.

What this means, in a behavioural finance context, is that although classification is very useful, and is essential for investment management and index construction, when one comes to decide on specific investments one has to dig deeper and study the facts and not rely on classification alone.

Winners and losers

We all know that reputations tend to stick. Once a person is considered a winner, success seems to follow. Unfortunately, too, the opposite is true if one gets a bad reputation, or is considered a loser.

You may be surprised to learn that this observation applies to companies as it does to people even though companies are continually analysed by investment analysts. While analysts do have a tendency to over-rate recent winners compared to recent losers, it is often the case that even when analysts change their opinions, investors are slow to change their minds and take up a previously underperforming stock. This is one of the factors on which event-driven hedge funds in distressed securities operate.

Change of opinion

"Usually, by the time that Wall Street analysts change their opinion from positive to negative on a stock, it is too late to benefit stockholders. How many times have you seen a company report surprisingly bad earnings, which causes the stock price to immediately drop, and *then* all the brokerage firms downgrade the stock? Or how about a stock falling from lofty levels – perhaps by as much as 50 percent – and then a brokerage firm downgrades it from 'buy' to 'hold'. Of what use is that to a short or intermediate-term trader? Thus, fundamental analysis may be more appropriate for the long-term picture, but it is not useful for short-term decision making."

McMillan on Options, Lawrence G. McMillan

The revenge of the losers

Two interesting studies by De Bondt and Thaler show that stocks that have been extreme losers in the preceding three years do much better during the next three years than stocks which have been extreme winners. The observation that past losers often shine unnoticed lies at the basis of investment strategies which recommend that investors invest in last year's dogs.

One such strategy is called Dogs of the Dow. Every year, an investor takes the 30 stocks of the Dow Jones Industrial Average Index and ranks them by dividend yield. The investor then selects the top ten yielding stocks. The shares with the highest dividend yield have a relatively low price and were last year's 'losers'. If, indeed, past losers often outshine winners, then these ten shares should outperform the other 20 in the forthcoming year.[4]

Dogs of the Dow has had positive, though mixed, results over the years.[5] This strategy can be worked out on any index, of course, including much bigger and more popular indices such as the S&P 500 in the USA or the FTSE 100 in the UK. It is usually applied to the Dow because it originated in the United States and, before the computer era, it was much easier to handle stocks in a small index. Also – a fact usually ignored in most of the literature – the Dow has a tendency to outperform the S&P 500.

Incidentally, Dogs of the Dow was popular much before behavioural finance took off. This shows that many investment strategies were based on old observations, which behavioural finance is now refuting.

Gambler's fallacy

Ask anyone the following question:

If I toss a fair coin, what are the chances of me getting a head?

Many would answer that I am likely to get a head about 50% of the time.

Indeed, the more often I toss the coin, the more I approach the magic ratio of 50 heads for every 50 tails.

But – *a big but* – this is only true *if I toss the coin a very large number of times*. If I only toss it ten times, I might find that I get eight heads and two tails, or three heads and seven tails. Once you read this, it is obvious – as 'obvious', in fact, as expecting to get a head 50% of the time.

---

[4] Some investment writers recommend the 'small dogs' version where one invests in the top five shares.

[5] A comprehensive website dealing with this strategy can be found at www.dogsofthedow.com. The website shows results for both the 'dogs' and the 'small dogs'.

This is one of those fascinating areas where there is a lot of slippage between risk, returns, expectations and common sense.[6] The important lesson is this: What is made valid by the law of large numbers is not necessarily true for small numbers.

This lands us directly between the jaws of the gambler's fallacy.

Let us get to an experxample.

I am tossing a fair coin and get the following results:

1st toss: head

2nd toss: head

3rd toss: head

4th toss: head

5th toss: head

6th toss: head

7th toss: head

Now, what's your gut feeling? What will I get on the 8th toss?

If you said "tails", you succumbed to the gambler's fallacy. If you argued that "a tail is now due" or that "it can't be a head again" or even started to doubt that the coin is fair, then you succumbed. The chances of getting a head on the 8th toss is still even.

In the gambler's fallacy we assume that the specific case we are looking at belongs to the set of large numbers and therefore should behave in a certain manner, that is, in the same way that units making a large number generally behave.

Once again, we are guilty of a representativeness bias. We think that this specific unit – the 8th toss of the coin – should somehow compensate for all the heads that came before it, by having a greater probability of coming up a tails. But it is the *class* which evens out, *not the individual*! And the representativeness bias, once again, gets us into trouble.

The subtlety of the gambler's fallacy

The gambler's fallacy can sometimes be very subtle, so we have to be especially alert for it. For example, a stock might start climbing because the company just registered a patent for a potion which revitalises men and women. Since we know that everything regresses to the mean and stocks fall as well as rise, we expect the stock to go back down sometime soon.

---

[6] For a fascinating history of how man struggled with understanding risk I recommend you read *Against the Gods* by Peter L. Bernstein.

We might be terribly disappointed! The stock might climb for years without an appreciable fall.

What applies to *stocks in general*, as a law of large numbers, might not be applicable to this particular stock at this particular time. We have succumbed to the gambler's fallacy by expecting the stock to fall.

Don't gamble, but if you have to, keep this in mind!

As one plays repeatedly and the number of tosses increases, the law of large numbers takes a progressively stronger grip.

If a casino has a 5% edge on its patrons, a patron who bets all he's got in small amounts is sure to lose. But a patron who throws all he's got in one big gamble might get lucky and carry off a big win.

In the long run, with small amounts, the edge delivers the beef to the casino. With one big bet, you might get lucky.

Magnification

We often make the opposite kind of mistake too and this second kind of mistake is part of representativeness bias as well, but works in the reverse direction: we often attribute the characteristics of a small group to the larger group.

We often assume that what we have observed about a small sample is representative of the whole population. This is sometimes called the law of small numbers, although it is actually the error of small numbers. Some authors refer to it as sample-size neglect since a sample has to be sufficiently large to make statistical inference valid.

There are numerous examples of this in real life. In finance it takes the form of:

Q: "Where do you think I should invest?"

A: "Oh, buy technology stocks. You know how well Microsoft and Google did over the years."

One cannot recommend a whole class just on the spectacular success of two members of that class. In making such erroneous inferences, one would be ignoring the small size of the sample.

The availability heuristic

In playing the experxample of tossing a fair coin (and maybe going for tails), we realised that what comes to mind first is not necessarily the right answer. Reasoned judgement is often very different from our automatic reactions.[7] We tend to be unthinking when making decisions on the go but get more logical when we have time to think.

The availability heuristic deals with the way we come to conclusions based not on statistical fact but on what most stands out from what is happening around us, with the images that are most readily available. We have often heard, or have given, the advice "you have to do with what you have." Well, this is exactly how our mind functions in using this heuristic to make decisions.

Experxample

What's more probable: being eaten by a shark or killed by a falling airplane?

I guess that ever since Stephen Spielberg directed *Jaws*, people have tended to opt for the first answer. Even more so if someone grew up swimming in the sea, as I did. The first image is much more dramatic and shocking than the second and it is therefore more available to the mind and is deemed more probable. In fact, you have more chance of being killed by a falling airplane than being eaten by a shark.

Another Experxample

What causes the most deaths, homicides or suicides?

Again, homicides are in the movies and in all the newspapers but we rarely hear of suicides. If you thought homicides was the answer, you were wrong.

---

[7] For more on this see *Blink: The Power of Thinking Without Thinking*, by Malcolm Gladwell.

> ### Another experxample
>
> What causes most deaths: hijacking of airplanes by terrorists, airplane crashes or car crashes?

An airplane crash is dramatic and a hijacking even more so. You've guessed right if you went for the last answer, by far.

We now realise, therefore, that what comes most easily to mind – because it is dramatic, shocking, and gets most media attention – is not necessarily the most statistically probable. The availability of the image plays havoc with our evaluation of risk.

The best investment fund there is

The availability heuristic is very powerful in financial services. One obvious example is mutual fund advertising.

Mutual fund companies advertise in media which are frequented by high net worth individuals (HNWI) and by investment advisers. As soon as HNWIs have cash earmarked for investment, who do you think will come first to mind? When an investment adviser is looking for a good performing fund to provide diversification to a client's portfolio, where do you think he will check first? They go to the heavy advertiser because its mutual funds are prominent in the mind's eye.

The advertising mutual fund company may not be the best there is and, even if the underlying portfolio is performing well, the extra charges supporting the advertising will pull it down a notch or two. Still, it is there dancing before prospective investors' eyes and is the one investors go to first. If an investment adviser recommends the advertised fund, the client is likely to already have heard about it.

Various studies have been made of closed-end funds. These funds, such as investment trusts in the UK, are often traded at a discount (sometimes even at a premium) to the value of their underlying portfolio of stocks. Closed-end funds often specialise in one investment area, such as a geographical region or a particular country. Studies showed that the good or bad news surrounding a country affects the discount or premium of a fund specialising in that country. The saliency of the news played an important role. Saliency was measured by the importance of the newspaper, the page on which the news appeared (the front page being the most influential), and the column width of the stories.[8]

---

[8] See for example the interesting study by Klibanoff, Lamont and Wizman, 1998, 'Investor Reaction to Salient News in Closed-end Country Funds,' *Journal of Finance* 53: pp. 673-700.

The recency bias

The recency bias is similar to the availability heuristic.

Under the influence of the recency bias, we tend to give more importance to, and consider more probable, events that occurred recently than those that occurred in the more distant past. Recent images are more available and, therefore, more influential.

Experxample[9]

A mutual fund performed about average between the year 2002 and 2005 but outperformed the index between 2006 and 2009. How do you expect it to perform in 2010?

One can never really know, of course, nor can we arrive at a proper forecast without studying a lot more about the mutual fund. However, given its good recent performance, it is reasonable to assume that 2010 will be a good year. The only basis for this guess is the fund's recent performance. So unless we have something more to go on with, we tend to stand on recent evidence.

In his very interesting book *The Education of a Speculator*, Victor Niederhoffer tells the story of his grandfather, Martin, who learned speculation under none other than the great Jesse Livermore. This was in the early 1900s and, after his training, Martin traded quite actively. Then, after the Depression, and the stock market crashes in 1929 and 1931, Martin grew anxious and started taking profits early, never riding gains more than 10 to 15 per cent above his purchase price, lest the stock market crashed again. He traded and invested under the shadow of the crash. His losses ate into his moderate profits. However, while anxiety walled Martin away from the big gains, the stock market did not suffer a big crash again for a long time – not until 1987.

---

[9] When approaching experxamples, relax. There is often no one right answer. And if there is, it is often not commonly known or apparent. Otherwise, what is the purpose of asking? Usually, in experxamples, the important thing is to gauge your initial reaction and thought processes.

Mind held hostage

Representativeness, the gambler's fallacy, the availability heuristic and recency bias can broadly be said to deal, in various ways, with our ways of putting some sort of order on the unknown. This imposed order, at least, gives us a framework within which to start thinking. If not knowledge, there is at least the *illusion of knowledge* and this gives us enough of an impetus to carry on and, hopefully, discover more.

We do not know enough about Linda, so we stereotype her. We do not know enough about a stock, so we attribute to it what is generally true of the class in which it belongs. We don't know which is the more common way to die, so we load it on the shark rather than a falling airplane part. We don't know which is the best fund, so we go for what we see most often in print or on TV. We don't know where the market is going, so someone could easily assume it is going down if they have just lived through the crash of 1929, or the 2007-2008 crisis for that matter.

But there are other ways in which our perception plays tricks on us.

Look at the following picture:

Figure 4.2: an open book

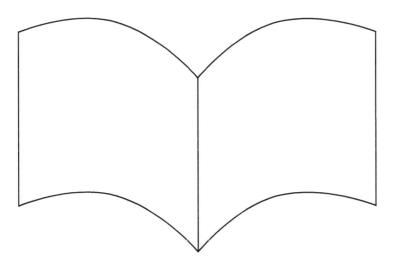

You can immediately tell that it is a book, or at least a pamphlet. But which way are you looking? Are you looking at the pages of an open book (is the book open towards you)? Or are you looking at the covers of a book open towards someone on the other side?

With this simple experxample we realise that we see and understand things *within a context*. Few things exist independently, in and of themselves. Someone is tall or short depending on the people around him or her. In Lilliput, I would be considered a giant; in Brobdingnag, pretty much a Lilliputian.

The brain, therefore, needs a context, or framework, and, in many ways, imposes limitations on itself. We often see things within the confines of these limitations. It is this observation which gave rise to the expression 'thinking outside the box'.

In addition to the framing bias, which we shall look at next, we shall also look at two other related limitations we place around our thinking; mental accounting and anchoring.

These three limitations are very important for the discussion of support and resistance levels in stock prices in Chapter Nine.

The framing bias

Diplomats know quite a lot about framing bias and that is why they take a lot of time in negotiating the agenda for important meetings between representatives of different states. The agenda frames the meeting and the conclusions reached in meetings often depend on the framework in which various items are discussed. If, during the meeting, someone raises an item which is not on the agenda, it is often chucked out. Such is the importance of the agenda, or frame.

Framing refers to the manner in which a rational choice is presented. The meaning of a question and the decisions made in answer to that question often depends on its context and the way it is put.

Framing often induces a reversal of preferences. Tversky and Kahneman demonstrated this via a series of experxamples known as the "Asian disease problem". In the experiment groups of physicians were asked to assume that the USA is preparing to combat an unusual Asian disease which is expected to kill 600 people. Alternative medical programme are proposed. Tversky and Kahneman showed that physicians' responses as to which programs they preferred depended on whether the question was framed around how many people will survive or around how many people will die.

The monk

A hypothetical conversation between a monk and a prior provides us with the epitome of framing. The monk asked the prior "Can I pray while I smoke?" rather than "Can I smoke while I pray?" The monk felt that smoking somehow reduced the solemnity of praying and, therefore, that the prior might object. On the other hand, he felt that praying always helps and that praying while one is smoking was commendable. He therefore framed the question that way.

Tailors

Framing goes to the root of how we think. There is the story of the two tailors in Savile Row, both of them called Cooper. It happened, by pure coincidence, that they set up shop next to each other on the Row. One of them put up a sign with "Cooper's Fine Tailoring" and the other one was about to put up a sign with something like "Cooper's Bespoke Suits" but, on second thoughts, came up with a much better solution, which framed the whole situation down pat. He put up a sign that said: "Cooper's Perfect Tailoring – Main Entrance". If you're walking down the Row looking for a tailor and you've heard of Cooper's, you're done.

Optimists, pessimists and investors

In general, when we say that someone is an optimist or that another is a pessimist we are referring to the context in which they frame their decision making.

With an optimist, adventure and risk are generally expected to lead to rewards while the pessimist sees only discomfort and losses. Whether to invest or not is therefore entangled in these general frameworks. The optimist is likely to invest and hope for the best while the pessimist tends to stay away from risk and leave his or her money in a bank account, which seems to be the safest alternative. As an investment adviser, I found that framing bias is one of the most common reasons why individuals make faulty decisions.

In this context, framing bias comes in two main forms:

1. Framing the performance of a portfolio in discrete time intervals, such as monthly, quarterly or annually.

Investors generally frame performance around portfolio statements. If an investor receives statements annually, he tends to look at performance over a whole year. If he receives statements every quarter, he tends to assess performance over three-month periods. If he receives a monthly statement, he adopts the month as the time interval. The investor might even decide to value the portfolio himself every Saturday. Maybe he has an online account and he can look at the value of his portfolio daily, even hourly.

Normally, if the investor adopts the right attitude, there is nothing wrong with frequent monitoring. What happens in practice, though, is that frequent reporting often brings with it anxiety and anxiety often leads investors to trade their securities more often than they should.

If one is investing for the long term, to supplement pension income, for example, then one should adopt a long-term time frame and look at things in a much longer framework than a day trader who needs to produce, if possible, profits every day. Someone investing for the long term need not bother with much of the information that is available daily but need only focus on a few important aspects of the portfolio.[10]

It is very important, therefore, that a long-term investor frames performance in the long term.

2. Framing performance around just one security, or one currency, in a portfolio.

Another common mistake is to concentrate too much on one aspect of one's portfolio.

At any time, a balanced portfolio is bound to have parts which are doing well and others which are performing poorly. One has to look both at the securities themselves and the currency in which they are denominated.

If one is investing for the long term and one part of the portfolio is suffering because the currency is falling in value, this does not justify liquidating the whole portfolio and withdrawing from investment in shares altogether. That part of the portfolio has to be framed within the wider context of the whole portfolio. We should not let that part of the portfolio become representative of the whole portfolio or representative of the advice one is receiving.

Frame it right

When checking performance, ask yourself three important questions:

1. What is my time frame?

2. What does my portfolio really consist of? Am I taking into consideration other portfolios I have with other firms? Am I taking into consideration other assets I own, such as my house?

3. Am I comparing my portfolio with the right benchmark? For example, comparing an international portfolio with, say, the S&P 500, is not the right way to go about it.

These three questions will help you frame your decisions in the appropriate context.

---

[10] Richard Bernstein, of Merrill Lynch, wrote a book about this aspect of investing. It is called *Navigate the Noise* and should be read by long-term investors attempting to keep an eye on their portfolio on a part-time basis.

The mental accounting bias

People have a bias whereby they categorise their assets into separate mental accounts. Economic outcomes are similarly categorised in the relevant mental account. The mental accounting bias, as it is called, is pervasive and stems, to some extent, from our framing bias.

The way we mentally account for money influences our behaviour, including our spending patterns. If a trader has a losing day, and he looks at that day on its own, the loss might make him risk averse and, in a bid to cut losses, he stops trading. Another trader who suffered the same loss, but looked at it in the context of a week's trading, or a month's, would probably have a different attitude, especially if he is lucky enough for this loss to be immaterial compared to the profit he made over the longer period.

We all remember the piggy banks we used to be given as children, to learn to put some money away. We were taught not to spend all that we received and to save some money for later, maybe to buy a big toy not otherwise procurable by coaxing or pleading. Gradually, too, we started making a distinction between income and capital. The capital has to be preserved while the income could be spent, less the amount saved.

These concepts are fundamental to finance. Shefrin and Thaler, for example, suggest that people allocate income over three classifications:

1. Current income

2. Asset income

3. Future income

People have the propensity to consume most from the first category and are reluctant to spend from future income even if it is certain to arrive. *Where* we allocate a cash inflow, therefore, determines *how* we actually spend it.

The house as an investment

Most of the behavioural finance literature deals with mental accounting as a bias, a departure from logic. Those involved with finance know that money is fungible: one pound is interchangeable for another, a quid pro quid. Treating money as nonfungible, therefore, seems to the financial mind to be somewhat illogical and mental accounting, which categorises wealth into different piggy banks, seems to be similarly illogical. And yet, there is a lot of sense, when examining one's finances, to attach different objectives and safeguards around each pool of money. Compartmentalisation may be illogical, but is often prudent.

A house provides shelter. You either own a house, and have shelter, or you have to pay for shelter, say by renting a house. For many people, for many years, the main benefit derived from owning a house was the shelter which came with it but, as house prices started to rise, especially in the ten years to 2007, many owners changed their mental accounting and started looking at their houses primarily as an investment asset. During a big part of that decade, the major monetary authorities kept interest rates too low and this fuelled house prices which, in turn, accelerated this shift in mental accounting.

People therefore borrowed against their houses and bought other things; some spent their money on merry making while others invested it, perhaps buying another house or two, and borrowing even more. The result of this shift in mental accounting was that when the price of houses broke, many could not afford the mortgage payments and lost not only their investment but often also their "free" shelter. While thinking outside the box is often illuminating, sometimes prudence requires an unimaginative approach.

Anchoring and adjustment

In his classic investment book *The Money Game*[11], written under the pseudonym Adam Smith, George Goodman tells us the story of Mr Smith:

> "Once upon a time there was a very astute gentleman we will call Mr Smith. Mr Smith was so astute that many, many years ago he invested in a company called International Tabulator. Mr Smith had great faith in the company, which in due course became IBM, waxed fat, and prospered. Mr Smith and Mrs Smith had children, and when they had grown up Mr Smith said to them, "Our family owns IBM, which is the greatest growth company in the world. I invested twenty thousand dollars in IBM and that twenty thousand has made me a millionaire. If something happens to me, whatever you do, don't sell the IBM."

Was Mr Smith right? Suppose it is 1997 and we are trying to decide whether to buy IBM for our portfolio.

Figure 4.3 is a graph of the IBM share price between early 1991 and mid-1997. The share price was at around $25 at the end of 1991 but then plunged to $10 in 1993. That's a 60% fall and it must have made Mr Smith roll in his grave.

Eventually, though, the share price went up to $53 by early 1997 and that is a 430% rise.

---

[11] This book exudes good humour and panache. What makes it a classic is its acute observations of investors and others in the financial arena. I have read it a number of times, at various stages in my career: when I was an accounting student, when I started out on my own as a financial adviser, later as an investment adviser very busy with client work and recently while writing this book. I always find a new, undiscovered angle each time I read it.

Figure 4.3: Share price of IBM 1991-1997

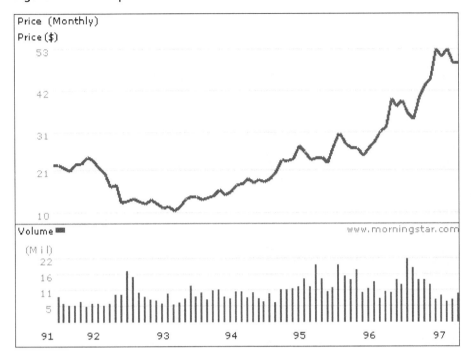

Well, now you are studying IBM to see whether you should take Mr Smith's advice and trust your hard-earned money on a stock which gyrates quite wildly. Would you buy IBM at around $50?

You might object and say that the Smiths and others had the benefit of a longer hindsight so, to be fair, let us trace the price back ten years further (Figure 4.4).

Figure 4.4: Share price of IBM 1987-1997

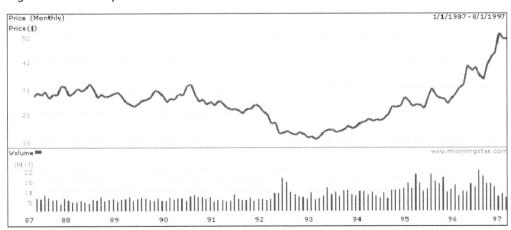

We now have a bigger picture and we know that the 1993 price of $10 was the lowest price reached during the previous ten years and that the price then gradually improved.

Whatever Mr Smith might have said, the $50 price in 1997 may look quite steep. Only four years earlier it was $10 and, during the last ten years, its best was around $30. You feel you should never pay more than $30, at most.

You call a friend of yours, a stockbroker, and he tells you that the prospects for IBM and technology companies in general were looking quite good and that $50 was a fair price to pay. You mention that you have had a look at the chart and that the price never went much above $30 and at one point it touched $10. He says that past prices reflect the difficulties the company and the market had but that past prices, especially those quite far away, should not be taken as a reliable guide for fair value today.

You mull over what your friend said and decide to adjust the price you had in mind. You now decide not to pay over $40. With the price around $50, you may well decide to go to the next share and not buy IBM – after all, Mr Smith is all fiction while your money was hard earned.

Now turn to the next page and look at Figure 4.5 to see how much would have been saved or lost by following this reasoning.

Figure 4.5: Share price of IBM 1997–2007

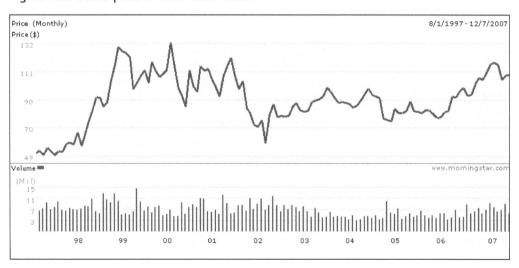

You thought $50 in 1997 was a steep price to pay! The share price shot up and touched $132, a 164% gain, before the tech stock meltdown in 2000. After that, the price climbed to $130 again in mid-July 2008 but was back to $80 at the end of 2008.

So, what have we observed about our behaviour?

On seeing the first graph, our mind was anchored on the $10, the lowest price reached. The importance we might have given to the $25 price was probably only as a reference point, to show how steep the fall was to $10.

When we saw the second graph, we got another reference price on which to tie the price, namely the $30 around which IBM moved between 1987 and 1991. We now have two reference points, or two *anchors* as they are called in behavioural finance, which help us put today's price in the picture.

The price in 1997, when we hypothetically had to decide, seemed much too high, at around $50. It was 'high' compared to the $30 or, even more so, compared to the $10.

We did not decide that the price was high by examining the fundamentals and making a proper valuation. We were looking at the $50 tag compared to what the price was in the past – a comparison such as we saw at the beginning of this chapter – and it looked too high. When our stockbroker friend told us that the price was fair, in his opinion, we were willing to pay more, but still in relation to the anchor prices. In other words, we were willing to adjust the price. But, as became evident later, we did not adjust enough, we only changed the anchor from $30 to $40.

In behavioural finance we see that, usually, adjustment comes too late and is too little. Our mind gets anchored to something – a figure, a stereotype – and sees reality in terms of that anchor. This is a demonstration of how the anchoring and adjustment bias, as it is called, operates in our minds.

Anchoring is extraordinarily powerful. Suppose that you were sitting in front of a spinning wheel of fortune. You were asked the percentage of African nations in the United Nations. When the wheel stops spinning the number ten comes up. You suggest that 25% of UN members are African. Surely, the number on the wheel – the ten – did not influence your choice of percentage, the 25%.

This was an actual experiment by Tversky and Kahneman. Surprisingly, it seems that the wheel number *does* influence the percentage figure you suggest even though it is unrelated and fortuitous. Tversky and Kahneman show that the median estimates were 25% for the group seeing ten on the wheel but that the median was much higher, 45%, for the group in front of whom the number 65 came up on the wheel.

There are many interesting experiments on anchoring and adjustment including one where it was shown that the listing price on a house for sale would influence even those who are expert at the valuation of real estate, even though only 8% of these experts admitted that they considered the listing price to be amongst the top three factors they take into consideration in their valuations.

Anchoring and adjustment plays a very important role in investment decision making.

Perception biases and investing

Decision making depends on how we perceive reality around us.

In investment, for example, we often notice that the strategies promoted at any one time by providers of financial services depend on what would have worked in the recent past. The strategies, therefore, depend on hindsight. But in financial markets, what would have worked in the recent past would not necessarily work in the near future. Hindsight is only of limited utility when we come to decide about the future.

Our financial decision making often depends on comparisons but we have to be careful that we are drawing the right conclusion. Not every emerging market is a China, not every internet company is a Google, nor is every energy company an Enron.

The representativeness bias often makes us decide by stereotype rather than by examining the real characteristics of a company or a situation – for example, it would be foolish for an investor to only invest in an innovative internet company if top management appeared sufficiently nerdy.

We saw how companies are usually classified in different categories on rather tenuous grounds. A value stock may provide good income while a genuine growth stock, really, is often a value stock. The way the categories are defined may often lead investors into errors resulting from the representativeness bias.

We often assume that what applies to large numbers and big samples also applies to small numbers and small samples. We encounter this when people buy a few stocks indiscriminately because the "market always goes up over the long term".

Investors also tend to base their financial decisions on what is ubiquitous and what is recent. Sometimes this helps them ride a trend as it forms but the availability heuristic and recency bias may make them invest in sectors which are overbought.

The way we see things depends on how they are framed and how our mind accounts for them. The idea that the "market always goes up over the long term" depends on which of the many markets we are framing and over what period of time. Our reaction to performance, or lack thereof, depends on the period of time we are framing and accounting for.

Finally, investment decision making – whether it be an individual investor deciding on whether to buy a stock or a securities analyst forecasting next year's earnings – often depends on where we started: the anchor. Opinions change in a series of adjustments from this anchor. If a share's price is now $5 and you started watching it when it was $2, it would seem expensive, unless it goes to $10 in which case your mind adjusts and $5 would seem cheap.

These perceptual factors must be kept in mind because they provide investors with both opportunities and pitfalls and as investors we are as susceptible to them as the next person!

Key concepts in this chapter

- Cognitive bias – hindsight
- Representativeness bias – the Linda experxample
- Conjunction fallacy
- Gambler's fallacy (law of large numbers)
- Sample-size neglect
- Availability heuristic
- Recency bias
- Framing bias
- Mental accounting
- Anchoring and adjustment

Chapter Five –
The Self: Tuum Est

"People travel to wonder at the height of mountains, at the huge waves of the sea, at the long courses of rivers, at the vast compass of the ocean, at the circular motion of the stars and they pass by themselves without wondering."

Saint Augustine

What this chapter is about

By nature, we have a strong sense of self and this influences our decisions, financial or otherwise.

Our brain carries within itself our whole history: likes and dislikes, people we met, our happy and sad times, attitudes, our medical history, and our expectations and hopes. This baggage is brought to bear on the way we see things, how we act, and how we make decisions. As agents of change, therefore, each of us acts and reacts depending on his or her past experiences and psychology.

Much like faces, no person's baggage is identical to any other's. Each of us are different and have had different experiences. Inevitably, we carry the self, and our *tuum est*[12], into the markets in which we participate. The markets, collectively, ultimately reflect what we are. It is our actions which ultimately power the invisible hand.

To put a limit and some order on what might be an unlimited topic, I am here going to look at three aspects of the self which impinge on our financial decision making:

1. Our inherent *optimism* and *pessimism.* Sentiment influences how much we are willing to pay to obtain something. What we decide before an event, and what actually happens once the event has taken place, results in a risk premium.

2. Our *openness to change.* Our conservatism, our under or over-reactions, and our overconfidence.

3. Biases which stem from our *egocentric* nature. We are subject to an endowment bias, believing that what we own is more important than what we don't. We tend to attribute success to ourselves and failure to others (self-attribution bias) and believe we are more in control than we actually are (illusion of control).

Always be an optimist, never a pessimist

As we saw earlier on in this book, risk taking is at the heart of investment and, therefore, is the prime driver of financial markets.

We as investors try to earn a higher than normal rate of return because we stake our money against an unknown future. We hope that by learning about markets and the

---

[12] These two Latin words are the motto of the University of British Columbia in Canada and mean *it is up to you* or, more strictly, *it is yours.* In one sense, it is up to you to make something of yourself and your life. In another sense, also, Tuum Est implies that a lot of things are up to you to interpret and decide upon. It is your brain which is processing the information which your senses gathered and you have to make up your mind which way to go. And you have to take responsibility for your actions.

psychology that drives them, we get a better understanding of what might unfold and a slight edge on other participants, and thus earn a higher return.

In order for us to be motivated to attach uncertainty to capital today, we must feel that there is a better future tomorrow. If not a better future for the lot of us, at least a better future for the asset in which we put our money.

So investors are naturally disposed to see the glass as half full rather than half empty, being optimists rather than pessimists, and while it is said that the only thing an optimist cannot see in a positive light is a pessimist, actually many optimists see an important role for pessimists in that the latter help curb foolish adventure. A Russian proverb, in contrast, states that a pessimist is a well-informed optimist.

Writers often link optimism and pessimism, which are emotional biases, to the investment style adopted by different managers, and specifically the so-called growth investors and value investors.

Growth vs value

Growth investors look for companies which can grow earnings faster than other companies. Figures of earnings growing at between 15% and 30% are often mentioned but these are just approximations – a lot depends on the circumstances, such as the industries, and the countries in which the company is operating. Growth stocks usually have a high price to earnings ratio and pay a low dividend, or none at all. If a company is growing its earnings at these handsome rates, investors would rather let the company use the money and forgo the dividend. There is a tendency for growth stocks to be more volatile and risky.

Value investors, on the other hand, head for the bargain basement and try to find companies which are trading at an attractive price compared to the assets the companies own and their earning potential. Value stocks tend to have low price to earnings ratios and often have a good cash flow and low growth opportunities and so tend to distribute more in dividends. The bargains value investors are looking for occur in various ways. The company may be at the low end of its business cycle, or it may have fallen out of favour, or there might be real or perceived difficulties, including an obsolete product. The dividends earned on such stocks tend to cushion falls but, unless carefully picked, such stocks may face lower earnings and have to cut dividends.

From the description of growth versus value investors one would assume that growth investors are the optimists while value investors are pessimists. However, some authors argue to the contrary. Growth investors, they say, are pessimists because they do not believe that growth in earnings would be widespread so they spend time looking for stocks which are likely to grow earnings and are willing to pay a good price for them. Conversely, value investors are optimists and believe that any fairly good company can make profits and they therefore concentrate on looking for reasonably priced companies. Value investors feel that if they buy at the right price, profits will follow, and they will then make a profit on their investment.

Of course, this is one of those problems caused by classification itself. Growth and value are two sides of the same investment decision. One has to arrive at an estimate of future earnings and cash flow and try to forecast how a company is likely to grow. Once one has discounted those earnings to the present, one has to look at various other matters. Of these, perhaps the most important are the price and the assets and liabilities, both tangible and intangible, which come along in the package of legal rights and obligations we call a company.

Buying at the right price is perhaps the most critical of all investment decisions. The assets and liabilities one is acquiring when one buys the stock are one's lifeline to the future, the link between one's investment today and what one is going to reap tomorrow. One cannot therefore look for growth and ignore the value of assets or vice-versa. The two approaches go hand in hand.

This practical approach to investment, combining growth and value evaluations, led to what is often called the GARP approach, growth-at-a-reasonable-price.

Perhaps the best known of the GARP strategies is the PEG system in which investors try to compare the price to earnings ratio (P/E) to the growth rate. A stock with a P/E of 20 and a forecasted earnings rate of 10% per annum, or a PEG of 2, is more expensive than a stock with a P/E of 20 and a forecasted earnings growth of 20%, in which case the PEG equals 1. A simplistic rendering of the PEG system would have one desist from buying a stock where the PEG is greater than 1.[13]

We can see, therefore, that investment strategies are built on behavioural foundations and we should try and be aware of these when we evaluate and classify investment strategies. One often meets the same things classified differently or seemingly different strategies which are based on the same behavioural concepts.

---

[13] I do not recommend the blind use of such an approach. Numerical cut-offs on financial metrics can profitably be used to make the computer do the donkey work involved in screening, but hardly ever work towards consistently good investment decisions except, perhaps, during the short time span when the cut-offs were determined. Markets change all the time and so should cut-off points. We have to acquire knowledge and interpret financial metrics dynamically, as circumstances change over time.

Before and after

In investment, we often focus on how we saw things before an event and what happened after.

Ex ante and ex post

"In times like these, it helps to recall that there have always been times like these."

Paul Harvey

When market participants are feeling generally pessimistic, all is darkness. They cannot see how companies will make money. All is gloom. There is no demand, or, if there is, liquidity is lacking. Nobody wants to hold stocks. Investors opt for other assets, such as bonds or property. The prices of stocks fall.

In such a scenario, before the event, *ex ante* in Latin, investors believe that they are going in for a bad spell but then, almost miraculously, a year or two later, it might turn out that profits were not actually as bad as they thought they were going to be. After the event, *ex post*, things may turn out much better than feared. The stocks which were derided last year start looking attractive.

This difference between what the market expects *ex ante* and what the market gets *ex post* is what creates the risk premium on assets. If everyone guessed perfectly what was going to happen, the risk premium would be zero because ex ante and ex post returns are identical.

If market participants are feeling generally optimistic, the world is good. They expect there to be profits for everyone, that earnings will increase without end, that there will be good demand supported by ample liquidity so that assets, including stock, would earn more and more.

In such a scenario, *ex ante*, many investors think that the returns from stocks would be much higher than from bonds and other assets. They are willing to pay more and more for stocks and the price rises. When earnings eventually disappoint, *ex post*, investors generally turn pessimistic. And so it goes on, with the market going up or down depending on the degree of optimism or pessimism in the market.

Measuring optimism and pessimism

There are many ways in which professional investors try to measure market sentiment and come to some conclusion as to overall optimism or pessimism of investors at any one time.

Methods include analysing newspaper headlines, and the words used (including the "R"-word, recession), surveys, analysing market and economic statistics, the number and volume of stocks going up versus stocks going down, the money value of these advances and declines, new highs and new lows, and option put-call ratios. A detailed treatment of these techniques belongs to another book. Here, I am just going to highlight one aspect of price as an indicator of sentiment.

One way to check whether market participants in general are feeling optimistic or pessimistic is to look at the level of prices in the market. If one is looking at the stock market, one can compare the market index today to the level of the index at various times in the past. It is important to check not just prices but market averages for such ratios as price to earnings, dividend yield, and price to book value. Such ratios contain indications as to how much optimism or pessimism is out there in the market.

Many investors get so caught up in the moment that they fail to make such simple but effective tests. You can learn a lot by simply comparing one year with another (while keeping in mind the pitfalls which comparisons sometimes involve).

If the market is frothy, for example, price to earnings ratios are high. This means that people are willing to pay a big multiple to buy future profits. Usually, when things are looking rosy, two mutually reinforcing levers start acting on the stock price. First, people start believing that profits are going to be higher than they previously thought they would be. Second, people would be willing to pay a higher multiple for these projected profits. The effect on stock prices of these two factors is extraordinary, as shown in this simple example.

Table 5.1: stock price movement in good times and bad

	Pessimism	Optimism
Expected earnings per share	$5	$7.50
Multiple	10	15
Stock price	$50	$112.5
Percentage change	––	125%

This illustration shows how a 50% increase in expected earnings per share – from $5 to $7.50, representing discounted future earnings – combined with a 50% increase in the rate at which market participants are willing to capitalise earnings, from a multiple of 10 to one of 15, leads to a change in stock price, not of 50%, nor even of 100%, but of 125%!

These two factors magnify each other to delight on the upside and shock on the downside. To reverse the example: in bad times, with poor sentiment, even if you invest in a relatively good company, which manages to earn $5 instead of the $7.50 it earns in good times, you can still see the stock price diving by 55% as the multiple falls from 15 to 10.[14]

Keep this in mind at any time you are investing in the market, but especially when you have bought a growth stock and it starts going awry – or when market sentiment is so negative that it fails to see earnings anywhere. Grasp this opportunity by buying good companies, unless you think things are likely to get even worse.[15]

Openness to change

The second aspect of the self which has a marked bearing on our financial decision making is our openness to change. Some people are naturally open to change and liberal while others want to retain the status quo and are by nature conservative.

We met the status quo bias, which is an emotional bias, earlier in Mr Smith's holdings of IBM. Mr Smith, whose twenty thousand dollar investment in IBM had made him a millionaire, used to exhort his descendants never to sell their IBM holdings.

The status quo bias is the tendency of people facing choice to hold on to how things are.

In my experience, I have found this to be quite a strong instinct. People do not like to change investments which worked in the past and, even if they intellectually understand the reason for a change, it takes time for them to become emotionally attuned to it.

---

[14] As I wrote this book, we were going through such a scenario. The gloom and the fear of worsening recession, if not depression, was hammering all shares, even those recently touted as recession proof, and even though earnings kept up quite well. Johnson & Johnson (JNJ), for example, hit $72 in September 2008, when it was being recommended as one of the safest stocks to be in and was now, six months later, at $50. The same with Wal-Mart (WMT), from $63 to $50. These shares did indeed do well relative to others but, in absolute terms, all stock prices suffer in times such as these.

[15] Many assume that the market is there to make them money. Actually, the market is there for companies and their advisers to sell paper to investors and for investors to get liquidity by being able to buy and sell paper to each other. The rights attached to this paper change all the time and, very often, investors do not have enough information to make the right decision. The market is not a game for amateurs. If you want to increase your chances of making a profit but can dedicate only a little time, make sure you stick your poles around a sufficiently small area so that you can master it completely. Amateur investors often try to achieve too much.

Conservatism

Related to the status quo bias, but usually considered to operate on the cognitive plane, is the conservatism bias. Conservatism makes people hold on to their previous opinions and forecasts even when new information indicates they should do otherwise.

We have already met conservatism in another form. In Chapter Four, while discussing the representativeness bias, we saw how people tend to form an opinion merely because something has similar characteristics to another and we noted how people tend to keep holding on to such an opinion even when it is apparent that it is no longer valid. We saw how reputations tend to stick, even to stocks, and how investors have the tendency to take their time to change their opinions, even investment analysts.

Later on we also saw how people form opinions via the process of anchoring and adjustment. One or two figures, sometimes grabbed from thin air, form the initial anchor and then, gradually, those estimates are adjusted depending on new information.

People are not machines. As new information arrives, they do not sit down with the proverbial blank sheet of paper and sharp pencil, study, contemplate, and work out the new odds. This is what they should do, perhaps, but not what they actually do. There is a reluctance to do the hard mental work required and there is also the emotional attachment to how things have been (the status quo bias). All of this makes people underrate and therefore underreact to news.[16]

The analytical capabilities of normal human beings, in contrast to the hypothetical powers of *rational economic man*, are rather limited. The brain often takes an emotional approach to problems, and emotion, while valuable, suffers from biases and errors. A common occurrence is that, after a series of underreactions, panic grabs us and we then tend to go to the other extreme and overreact.[17]

At a basic level we saw how the human brain seems to be better at understanding frequencies rather than probabilities. We are often willing to settle for rough averages rather than take the trouble to do the actual arithmetic. At a higher level, statistics and statistical concepts are often hard to grasp and analyse. It is surprising how complex the analysis of even a rather simple set of data quickly becomes.

---

[16] Incidentally, the reluctance of many top executives to get their hands dirty and get busy with a calculator and a sharp pencil often lies at the root of poor supervision which makes it easier for corporate fraud and gross negligence to take place. The devil, as they say, is in the details.

[17] Underreaction and overreaction are fruitful areas of both behavioural finance research and investment management.

Forecasting

One would expect that professional forecasters, such as securities analysts, would somehow control and adjust for these biases.

Studies have shown that, often, many analysts simply get it wrong. Reality anticipates forecasts rather than the other way round. Dreman and Berry, for example, studied 500,000 individual earnings predictions by securities analysts on Wall Street and found that the average forecast error was 44%.

Analysts have been found to be conservative, to underrate the importance of the new figures, and therefore to underreact by not changing their forecast quickly and far enough. Forecasts therefore lag behind reality. And this generally applies for both stock and bond analysts. The biases of *representativeness, anchoring and adjustment*, and *status quo* may also be involved. These biases often come to play in the dynamic processes involved in trying to guess what will happen tomorrow.

But there is something wrong here!

Why does someone who gets it wrong the first time not adjust his or her thinking, but instead continue in the old ways and persist in underrating news and underreacting to it? Partly, it is a result of an analyst not wanting to stick his or her head out by being too different from other analysts.[18] But there is often more than this.

Overconfidence bias

The answer may lie in that many people are not only conservative but overconfident in their abilities.

In other words, there is an overconfidence bias which makes people think they are better than they actually are. Overconfidence gives conservatism momentum and seems to lead to the observed lag of forecasts to reality.

As an aside, before we continue, I wish to emphasise that forecasting successfully is far from easy. One has to construct and attach probabilities to a range of future scenarios and try to decide which figures are the most likely. Even if one managed to throw away all the psychological biases, and morph into an REM, the task would still be quite daunting. We wish that forecasts were better but the shortfall to expectations is not surprising, especially for those who have tried securities analysis and forecasting.

---

[18] The pressure on an analyst like Ms Meredith Whitney, who focused investors' attention on Citigroup's capital shortfall, must have been tremendous.

Egocentricity

Not surprisingly, our third topic, egocentricity, plays an important role in behavioural finance.

We saw when discussing the conservatism bias how people have the tendency to hold on to their opinions and we saw that this stems from the status quo bias, an emotion which makes people hold on to the way things are. In a similar way, people often value an asset more when they have it than when they do not. The fact that they have something makes them think it is more important and valuable than they would objectively have done if they did not have it. This is called the endowment bias.

Rational economic man would pay a given amount of money to acquire something and would be willing to sell that same object for an equal sum of money. Not so most of us. Once we acquire something, it often takes on a higher value in our minds and we are reluctant to let it go at the market price. This is an emotional bias.

One implication of this is that we often try to avoid trading at market prices and this feeds a tendency to buy and hold. The price never seems to be high enough for us to part with our stock, as in the IBM example from *The Money Game*.

As a result, we would not want to face news which somehow reduces the value of what we hold. Bad earnings are excused or considered to be just an exception. If bad management takes control of the company, we start finding excuses for them, or, if not, we hope they're discovered and replaced soon. Dreams and hopes colour what we have and make us reluctant to face the facts. As we saw, we would then underrate bad news, overrate good news, and overreact or underreact.

The stock one minute before we bought it is most probably the same as the stock one minute after but once we start thinking of the stock as our stock, it will start looking much more comely. After all, *we have chosen it*. We now have an endowment, a vested interest. The endowment bias may lead to decision paralysis, rendering decisions impossible. We just hold on and hope. The market price is never good enough.

Experienced traders and investors train themselves to guard against endowment bias. They train themselves to look at news in the face, try to adjust their anchor price as soon as the facts justify the revision and are willing to trade at market prices. They are more REM-like in their approach.

Self-attribution bias

The reader should notice that most of the biases discussed in this chapter are easy to understand and are rather intuitive, stemming directly from what makes us human beings. Another such is the self-attribution bias.

The self-attribution bias, as its name implies, refers to our cognitive tendency to ascribe success to ourselves and failure to others, to outside influence, such as astrology, or bad luck. When we are successful we have a tendency to be happy with ourselves and credit our intelligence or great efforts for the results. This leads to overconfidence, over-trading, taking on too much risk, and ultimately failure. On the other hand, we tend to put failure at other people's doors, or to blame outside factors.

Another cognitive bias is the illusion of control. People tend to feel that they control the outcome of events. The illusion of control makes people feel empowered and very confident and must therefore be recognised for what it is – an *illusion* – and held in check. "Don't confuse brains for a bull market", the adage warns. In some cases, this illusion gets wound around various rituals and superstitions which may even have pathological consequences if taken to extremes.

People's expectation of success can go beyond what the objective probabilities would suggest. Ironically, this belief can feed the optimism that makes people undertake great journeys of discovery or other entrepreneurial endeavours. It is one of those quirks in human nature which makes certain individuals take on the unknown.

We can see, therefore, how these three examples of egocentric biases often power other biases identified by behavioural finance. We often hear expressions such as those in the following box in this context. They must, however, be recognised for what they are and not be allowed to interfere unduly with rational decision making.

Example: statements about stocks and the biases they reveal

"I am not letting go of these shares for less than I bought them for."

- Endowment bias
- Vested interest

"I will hold this stock till I die."

- Buy and hold

"I have to cut my losses but then that means I was wrong in the first place."

- Decision paralysis

"I knew this stock was great. The other one, the one I took a loss on, I got from TV."

- Self-attribution bias

"I know all about this stock, don't worry."

- Illusion of control

Investing and the self

Our optimism or pessimism obviously plays a major role in our investment decision making. Observing whether other participants are optimistic or pessimistic, or maybe even excessively so, provides us with many investment opportunities.

Indeed, the main concept behind behavioural technical analysis, which we shall examine in Chapter Nine, is to try and ascertain the main behavioural finance factors at play in the market at any one time in order to put them to use in making profitable investment decisions. If we detect over-optimism, for example, maybe it is time to sell. If we see excessive pessimism, it may be time to buy. Our investment decisions are often judgement calls on what we think is going on in the market.

The self often plays a subtle role: one investor may be open to change and overconfident while another may be conservative and hesitant. An interesting area of study is over reaction and under reaction to news and these reactions often lead to either a switch from optimism to pessimism (or vice-versa), or to an intensification of either.

Once an investment decision is made, investors tend to become wedded to that decision and experience an endowment bias. They attribute any success to themselves, and failure to others. They also feel more in control, and more knowledgeable, than they actually are. Such may be the extent to which investors suffer from decision paralysis.

Key concepts in this chapter

- Optimism and pessimism

- Ex ante, ex post, risk premium

- Openness to change

- Conservatism

- Underreaction and overreaction

- Overconfidence

- Egocentric

- Endowment bias

- Decision paralysis

- Self-attribution bias

- Illusion of control

Chapter Six –
Aversion: Pursuing Pleasure And Avoiding Pain

"One of the things I did when I was ten or eleven years old, I read every bit of financial history I could because it isn't just about the figures on the chart last week, it's about how human beings behave."

Warren E. Buffett (Interview with Charlie Rose, May 2007)

What this chapter is about

In many ways, this chapter is the centre of the book, treating the most important concepts in behavioural finance and bringing together various strands of thought. It also deals with prospect theory, around which much behavioural finance work is built.

The chapter begins with Freud's pleasure principle and then goes on to deal with our aversions. The first is our aversion to ambiguity and this leads us to a discussion of risk and uncertainty. We are averse to regret and, certainly, to loss. Each of us seems to have his or her risk habitat and would like to stay there, venturing out only if it means we gain something meaningful.

If there are losses, we tend to want to get even and if we have invested in a winner we have the tendency to sell it (the disposition effect).

Much of what we have discussed so far in this book comes together in prospect theory where we see that our decisions when making gains are different from our decisions when making losses. Prospect theory, so far, is probably the key insight of behavioural finance.

The pleasure principle

This chapter is really about the pleasure principle. This concept was developed by Sigmund Freud and is rather simple, as all great concepts are. The pleasure principle makes us seek gratification, motivating us to seek pleasure and avoid pain.

Profit is usually a pleasure while loss is painful. In the previous chapter we saw how this profit-seeking motive made people want to invest and therefore moved markets. Profit-seeking is motivated by the pleasure principle. The most important work in behavioural finance involved the application of the pleasure principle to the way people make financial decisions.

In this chapter, we shall start by looking at our aversions, what we seek to avoid. We shall approach this topic by in turn looking at stronger and stronger aversions.

We do not like *ambiguity*, with a rather mild sort of aversion. But we surely do not like *regret*, with an even stronger aversion. And we definitely hate the pain of *losses*, with the strongest aversion of them all.

What will the future be?

Knowing too much will often land you in trouble. In Alfred Hitchcock's 1957 movie, *The Man Who Knew Too Much*, the hero of the story, Dr Ben McKenna, was informed by a dying spy that a certain head of state was going to be killed. To keep McKenna from revealing what he knew, his son was kidnapped by the assassins and he went though various torments until, at last, he reached a sort of information equilibrium, and did not know too much.

Ironically, while knowing too much can be fatal, the movie is usually remembered for the Doris Day song "Que Sera, Sera", or "Whatever Will Be, Will Be" about a girl who wanted to know more, not less, but who, as a woman, realised that the best way forward is to just let the future be.

This example captures the eternal human dilemma with the future. Does the future exist? Is the future knowable? Should one try to peek into the future? Does looking into the future somehow attract bad luck? If one does get to know the future, what can one do about it but wait for the future to unfold?

We often give up and, like Doris Day, say "whatever will be, will be," but this does not diminish our anxiety about the future and our ambiguity aversion.

In behavioural finance ambiguity aversion, a cognitive bias, is studied in some depth because ambiguity is *a disincentive to risk taking.* Facing uncertainty, we often stop dead in our tracks, to think about the situation, to try and figure out the odds and build courage. Indeed, breaking down the barriers created by ambiguity aversion is often the first step in entrepreneurship and other forms of risky endeavours.

Risk and uncertainty

Ambiguity plays an important role in finance. The discussion of rational economic man in Appendix 1 shows that economic decision making often revolves around expected utility and we assumed that the probabilities attached to each outcome are known. In tossing a coin, for example, I know that my chances of getting a head or a tail are 50%, provided the coin is a fair one. But what are my chances of making a profit or a loss if I buy 100 shares of Microsoft today? There is a probability associated with each outcome but I do not, a priori, know what that probability is.

In finance, therefore, we often make a distinction between *risk* and *uncertainty*. In a risk situation, we know what the probabilities associated with each outcome are, like in the case of the fair coin. Under uncertainty, we do not have this knowledge and we are exposed to ambiguity.

Finance and investment – their classification, analysis and forecasting – can be seen as a struggle with risk and uncertainty. We have applied mathematics to markets in a bid to unravel their behaviour today so that we can forecast their behaviour tomorrow. We are rather good when it comes to the analysis of risk situations. If we consider risk analysis, and take options as an example, we find that we can price options by using the Black-Scholes model or the Cox-Ross-Rubinstein binomial model, where we are assuming that the price of a security moves up or down in accordance with certain probabilities.[19] We also know that trends tend to persist and we know that there is usually reversion to the mean, which means that trend followers and contrarians are hard at work. But when it comes to dealing with uncertainty, where no probabilities are assumed, we are at quite a loss.[20] Indeed, the big objective in finance is to transform uncertainty into risk so that it can be managed and put to use creating wealth.

One of the main causes of the present financial crisis is that mathematical models led financial firms, including banks, to take on uncertainty, thinking they were taking on risk, and credit was allowed to mushroom. For a long time, rubbish was sold and bought in the guise of solid securities.

Ambiguity aversion is not irrational. It is engendered by the unknown and, rather than ignore it, the best we can do is try to cope with it. One effect of our ambiguity aversion, for example, may be to stay at home and invest in our own economies where we know how things work rather than venture out and invest in other economies. This, however, restricts our horizons and limits our opportunities. A preferable response may be to research other markets, reducing uncertainty, and then diversify.

Ambiguity aversion also helps to guard against black swans – one-off, highly improbable, but possible, events.[21] While most swans are white, there is the rare black swan. An investor has to be on guard for the unexpected rare event, the fluke. The black swan shatters the false comfort engendered by probability distributions.

---

[19] For a binomial model, for example, we can assume that today's $100 price has a 60% chance of moving to $101 by tomorrow and a 40% chance of moving to $99, and then project forward a tree, with two branches at each node, far into the future. We can then work out where the price is likely to be in a month's time. There are also trinomial and quadrinomial formulae in use, giving rise to more branches and complicated trees and sophistication.

[20] Note that even fractal geometry, the so-called geometry of chaos, assumes the recursion of certain pre-defined patterns. Patterns, however, do not always recur identically. Monte Carlo simulation is an effective tool that, in its pure form, assumes randomness. We know, however, that while there is almost no correlation between a security's returns for different days – implying randomness – there is statistically significant positive autocorrelation between the *magnitude* of returns in nearby days and that periods of high and low price volatility tend to cluster. This tallies with human behaviour.

[21] See *Fooled by Randomness* and the more recent *The Black Swan* by Nassim Nicholas Taleb.

Regret aversion

Regret aversion plays a major role in financial decision making. As its name implies, this is the fear that, in the future, we might regret today's decision. As a result, we do nothing.

We all know how regret aversion works. It is often a two-edged emotional sword if only because doing nothing is itself a decision. Regret aversion often also leads to opposite reactions. Let us have a look at some examples.

Regret aversion in practice

- Tom has noticed how financial company stocks fell once credit problems came out in the open. He thinks that financial company stocks offer great value now, after such steep falls. Tom does not buy financial stocks because he reasons that, should he buy and subsequently make a loss, he would regret his decision – he had been forewarned by the previous losses.

- Kathy is the great-granddaughter of Mr Smith and still has her IBM stocks. She sits on a huge amount of capital gains but would not sell the shares because if she did and the shares continued to do well, she would regret the decision all her life. She would feel especially bad if she spent the proceeds or invested them poorly.

- Peter is a computer buff. In 1994, he bought 1000 shares of Microsoft at around $3 each. By early 1998, the shares had more than sextupled in value, to $20 each. This was the nicest $17,000 he ever made. In 1998, Peter had a mortgage and a young family. Although he still liked the company and thought it had a great future, he sold the shares because, he reasoned, he would really regret it should the stocks fall. (Microsoft shares peaked at $59 in 1999.)

- Monica notices that corporate bonds usually give better returns than certificates of deposit. Her investment adviser suggested she put some of her sizable savings in high quality bonds but when Monica learned that even investment grade bonds can default she conservatively decided to leave all her savings on deposit because she did not want to regret her actions.

- Gerald invested in a biotechnology company which owned several patents. At first he made a profit on the stock but then the company stopped coming out with new patents and the ones it had were expiring or being rendered obsolete by new inventions. Gerald hoped that the situation would turn around and that maybe the company had some aces up its sleeve. Selling the stock seemed to him to be tantamount to giving up on the company and admitting that the investment was a mistake. Gerald decided to hang on to the shares to avoid the regret which comes with being a quitter. He also reasoned that the company may one day play its aces and come back – he would then surely regret that he had sold early.

• Mary had some 'risk money' to invest but she did not really follow the stock market. At the end of one particular month, when she once again was reminded of the extra money in her bank account, she decided that she had to put the money to good use that very week. The best way to invest is to follow the crowd, she thought, because they cannot be all wrong. She opened a lifestyle magazine and saw an advertisement saying that smart investors have traditionally invested in gold. She decided to invest in stocks of a gold mine. She reasoned that if it proved to be a bad investment, she was in great company. "It is not as if this was my idea," she said to herself as she signed the cheque. By following the crowd and avoiding any personal input, Mary was attempting to protect herself against regret aversion and hedging herself against regret in future should her investment in gold go wrong[22].

We can see from the examples that avoiding regret is often very difficult whatever one does or does not do.

Freud's second principle

Curiously, in my experience with investment clients I noticed that people often tend to do nothing rather than risk doing the wrong thing. Maybe this is because an error of commission seems worse than an error of omission; wrong things we have done seem more painful than things we missed out on. Actually, whether by commission or omission, an error is an error.

While regret aversion is natural, as investors we should learn to identify it immediately for what it is and try to avoid making wrong decisions simply because of this emotional bias.

Freud's second principle, the reality principle, comes in useful in this regard. It states that as we mature we realise that, in the real world, pain is often necessary to eventually achieve pleasure: "An ego thus educated has become *reasonable*; it no longer lets itself be governed by the pleasure principle, but obeys the reality principle, which also at bottom seeks to obtain pleasure, but pleasure which is assured through taking account of reality, even though it is pleasure postponed and diminished."

So, as investors we should not opt for inaction when we feel we should act just because there is pain associated with regret.

---

[22] Investment advisors know this kind of protection and hedging by clients very well. It is most apparent when clients hand over money to their advisers without wanting to know anything about the recommended investment and usually telling their advisors, "I leave all this up to you."

Loss aversion

In Chapter Five we discussed the status quo bias and the conservatism bias. The status quo bias is emotional and causes people to hold on to how things are. The conservatism bias is cognitive and causes people to hold on to their previous opinions and idea frames even though facts have changed.

The conservatism bias, therefore, is one of the main supporters of the status quo bias. We want to retain the status quo and we refuse to look at new facts and change our opinions. The status quo engenders contentment, a sense of protection and belonging, which is why we want to hold onto it. In order to protect the status quo we have to avoid losses and, therefore, we have a bias towards loss aversion. But it goes further. The fact that we feel pain when we incur a loss – whether we consciously want to preserve the status quo or not – means that loss aversion also encourages the status quo bias.

Status quo, conservatism and loss aversion are mutually reinforcing. After all, change means risk and risk means the possibility of loss – while trying to avoid a loss we shirk risk. This works towards preserving the status quo. If the status quo was perfect this would be a good thing but often we find that we need change to improve things.

Status quo satisfaction hypothesis

It seems, therefore, that if we are not satisfied with our status quo, then we are likely to be risk-seeking. We would be willing to bet more, perhaps even bet against the odds, to get out of the state we are in. If we are satisfied with our status quo, then we are likely to be risk averse. One would have to offer us very good odds for us to play because we are comfortable where we are. Let's call this the status quo satisfaction hypothesis.

Figure 6.2: Status quo satisfaction

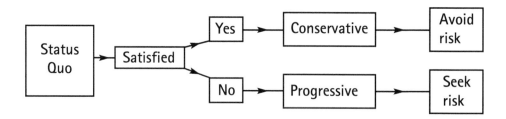

We see this behaviour every day. If stock markets are booming, one has to increase interest rates to tempt people away from their status quo in equities.

Get-evenitis

In finance, loss aversion has very important consequences. One of these is the so-called get-evenitis effect. Instinctively, we all know how it works. Often, it leads to massive losses and can be hazardous to our wealth. We hope against hope, as we say, and our losses mount until we are left with nothing.

We buy $10,000 worth of stock in company ABC which had just published a press release saying that it is in the final stages of applying for patents for an edible substance which will serve both as a food and a beverage, an organic and non-fattening substance in keeping with today's dietary preferences, cheaper than bread and water, nourishing and with a balance of all the vitamins and minerals so important for a healthy life, and, what's more, you'll never get tired of the taste. A modern day manna.

The shares in ABC are in great demand and they rise in expectation of the company acquiring the patents and journalists storm its offices to try and get a likely time frame for the products development. ABC eventually issues another press release saying that, while its research is progressing as scheduled, and that every indication shows that the substance will more than satisfy all of the company's promises, the company had decided to embark on a rather lengthier testing period to ensure the highest quality standards possible.

Investors who stayed on the sidelines, growing sceptical as time went by, now buy some shares. Existing investors take courage and, since they already have a sizable profit, feel they could afford to wait for higher gains. The price rises and our stake is worth $60,000.

Days, weeks and months go by and there's no more news from ABC. Some of the first investors get impatient and fear they will lose their profit, and so start selling shares. The price starts to ease.

There is then a regulatory filing and another press release. The board of ABC has fired the CEO because the board felt that he did not fully appreciate the importance of moving quickly to file for the patents. The CEO was well-regarded and the share price falls some more.

We hold on to our shares because we have faith in ABC and in the board's decision to get a more dynamic CEO. Another month goes by, then two. The share price keeps weakening. ABC is no longer communicating with the press.

Then there is a regulatory filing stating that the second CEO has resigned. When questioned, the chairman of the board confirms everyone's fears: that ABC has no actual timetable for filing the patents.

By the time we find a quote screen, our holding in ABC is worth $7000. All our profits are gone, and we made a $3000 loss. We kick ourselves for not taking our profits when we had the chance. We curse the new CEO and discuss what we're going to do. No way are we taking a loss on this! What if this CEO left for something other than a defective product? What if the share price shoots up in a couple of days? We decide to grin and bear it, hoping that this is all a bad dream, praying that ABC does actually start producing its product, so that we eventually at least get even, and do not make a loss.

The disposition effect

As every investor and stock trader knows, as soon as you take a position, you get anxious. This anxiety, along with loss aversion, leads to what Shefrin and Statman call the disposition effect: investors have a tendency to sell winners too early and keep losers too long. We have seen the second aspect – clinging on to losers – in the preceding example, as a manifestation of the get-evenitis effect. The first aspect though, selling winners too early, is equally interesting.

Holding on to losers – and failing to mitigate losses by getting out of a security while the loss is still small – usually results from false hopes and the reluctance to add finality to a loss-making decision. By postponing finality we also hope to avoid regret.

Selling winners too early is often due to our getting anxious of losing the profit we have built up. We do not want to postpone taking profit and then have to live with the regret of losing this profit should the price of the security turn against us.

Finally, investors who dispose of winners are usually anticipating that prices revert to the mean, as they usually do. If prices revert, they will lose their profit, or part of it, and many investors often cash in.

Small losses, big profits

"Take your losses early and let your profits run" is a well-known adage, easy to understand but, as often is the case in investment, difficult to practise. It takes training and self-control to be able to quash false hopes as they arise and to control anxiety as it builds up along with paper profits. It is also said that "one never goes broke by taking a profit," but if you are taking small losses and small profits you get nowhere – one should try and take small losses and big profits.

The disposition effect illustrates how good investment practice often goes against the emotional grain. Investors have to do what is logical rather than what is emotionally appealing. This is why good investment is often as much about nerves as about intellect. Whatever investment method is used, it is bound, at one time or another, to cause distress and, at that point, having verified the facts and made all enquiries, one has to hold on to what one believes is valid.

Unfortunately, the nature of the market does not help. Markets tend to fall rapidly when fear takes over and grind up slowly when greed has the upper hand. This implies that one has to be rather quick on the trigger to stop a loss from escalating and must possess quite a lot of stamina to sit on unrealised profit.

Prospect theory

In what is perhaps the single most important paper in behavioural finance, Kahneman and Tversky showed that not only do people have a loss aversion bias but that they also actually treat gains and profits differently. This was a very important observation.

Prior to their paper, in accordance with the expected utility theory (discussed in Appendix 1), economists assumed that profit was as pleasurable as loss was painful and that a person would want to take risk depending on the probability attached to expected gain or loss. If a profit of $1 led to a pleasure of x, then a loss of $1 was assumed to cause an equal and opposite pain of x. Kahneman and Tversky, however, found that this neat system does not hold in reality.

First, let us see how people react to risk of loss by considering an experxample in a similar vein to those designed by Kahneman and Tversky.

Experxample: facing a certain profit

You have $300.

You now have a choice between:

1. Receiving another $100, or

2. Tossing a coin, where if you win you get $200 and if you lose you get nothing.

What would you choose?

In such an experxample, actually conducted by many researchers, it was found that the majority choose option (1) rather than (2), even though the expected winnings in (1) and (2) are identical, if we merely look at expected utility.

Let us now look at a second experiment.

Experxample: facing a certain loss

You have $300.

You have a choice between:

1. Giving up $100, or

2. Tossing a coin and paying out $200 if you lose or nothing if you win.

What would you choose?

This time, the majority of respondents preferred (2) to (1), even though, again, the expectations in both (1) and (2) are identical.

It can be observed that while the subjects in the first experxample, *facing a certain profit*, opted to *avoid risk* by choosing a sure, though smaller, gain over an uncertain one. In the second experxample, *facing a certain loss*, most subjects chose *to go in for risk*, going for an uncertain big loss over a certain small loss.

The attitude can be paraphrased as: if it means gaining, let me make sure. If it means losing, let me take a chance.

The pleasure principle, again

At the most basic level, this observation ties in with the pleasure principle. Various research studies have looked at the affect associated with various stimuli. The affect is the good feeling or the bad feeling which we feel after we receive a stimulus. The word gold, for example, generates a positive feeling while the word abyss provokes fear and a negative feeling.

Prospect theory shows that investors are risk averse when facing gains but risk seeking when facing losses. The positive affect investors feel towards gains engenders within them a negative affect towards risk; the negative affect investors feel towards losses makes them look favourably at risk. But prospect theory goes further to explain why people switch between risk taking and risk avoidance depending on the outcome.

Kahneman and Tversky's insight analysed

One could argue that if expected utility theory held, in both experxamples, people would have been indifferent between going for (1) or for (2). The fact that they have chosen to go for (1) in the first experxample and to go for (2) in the second means that people contemplate sure gains and sure losses differently.

In the case of a sure gain, we don't want to take chances and play. In the case of a sure loss, we want to play and risk. While all this confounds logic, it seems a perfectly natural way for someone to behave. Why? Some reasons:

* We do not normally think in terms of how much *total wealth* we would have *after* the game is over ($400, $500 or $300 in the first experxample; $200, $100 or $300 in the second) but in terms of *gains* or *losses*, that is, *in terms of changes*. We already discussed this in Chapter Three where we noted that we have a tendency to look at *change* rather than *maintained states*. In these experxamples, most people think in terms of the $100 or $200 gains or losses, the changes to their wealth.

* In the experxamples we again have the idea of our *status quo*, discussed in Chapter Five. The experxamples start by telling us how much we start off with. We then tend to see the gains and the losses – the changes – in terms of this status quo.

* Kahneman and Tversky found that people underweigh outcomes that are merely probable versus outcomes that are certain. This is called the certainty effect. This has to do with the bird in the bush scenario in that nothing beats certainty. Professor Richard Zeckhauser explains the certainty effect by means of an interesting example. The experxample derived from the professor's model can be seen in the following:

Experxample

A person is playing Russian roulette. The gun has four bullets with two chambers left empty.

If you were that person, how much would you be willing to pay for the referee to take out one bullet and reduce the chances of the gun firing from 67% to 50%? Write the answer down.

Next, how much would you pay to have another bullet taken out, thus reducing the chances of the gun firing from 50% to 33%? Please write down the answer.

Next, how much would you pay to have another bullet removed, reducing the chances from 33% to one-sixth or 17%? Please write down the answer.

Finally, this person has one bullet left. The chance of it firing is quite low, at 17%. If you were that person, how much would you pay to have the final bullet removed and live to see another day? Again, write down the answer.

In the first instance, reducing the probabilty by 17%, from 67% to 50%, is quite meaningful but at 50:50 the person still has a big chance of being unlucky. The same goes to taking out the second bullet and reducing the probabilty to a third. But when it comes to the final 'life and death' bullet, it is natural to assume that one would be willing to pay much, much more. That final bullet gives the person *certainty*.

There is another factor, called the *isolation effect*, which I mentioned in Chapter Three, and which plays a rather minor role in Kahneman and Tversky's work. They note that in making decisions people tend to discard components common to all prospects under consideration.

Thus, if you're looking at cars, they all come with four wheels in place and one spare, so when you see the next car and it has its wheels in place this fact is unlikely to be a decision factor. But if you see a car without wheels and the salesperson tells you that you have to buy the wheels elsewhere and put them on yourself, you start looking at this fact in isolation and wheels suddenly become a big factor in your decision and this may easily put you off the car.

Prospect theory notes that the isolation effect may result in inconsistent preferences when the same choice is presented in different forms. In this case, maybe the rational decision would have been to buy the wheels elsewhere and go for the car.

I once came across this when I ventured to buy a car of a well-known brand. The salesman told me that the interior mats were not included in the hefty price. That forced me into an inconsistent preference, and I lost interest in the car. Although, for other reasons which became apparent later, I never regretted my decision, my decision process, looked at on its own merits, was faulty.

The value function

All these concepts come together in prospect theory, the essence of which is perhaps best captured in the value function.

In order to best understand the value function, let us take a life-like example.

A hypothetical example to illustrate the value function

Early one morning, you are lying in bed, feeling secure and lazy, and you decide to tot up your wealth. You estimate that it amounts to $1 million. You get out of bed, shower and go down to breakfast. Once you're done, the telephone rings. It is John, a friend of yours. He suggests that you partner with him in a real estate venture. He tells you that you stand to gain $100,000. You ask him about the downside and he says that you have to put in $100,000 and that you might lose it all. You thank him for calling but decline to be his partner. John is persistent and says that he would really like you to join him as his partner. You then say that you do not like the odds as he stated them and that in order to join he has to offer you a sweeter deal. He says he cannot do much on the upside but can do something about the downside. John asks you what potential loss you would be able to live with for a $100,000 gain. You say that you won't put on the line more than $25,000. John says that's tough but that he'll think about it and let you know.

The situation explained by prospect theory

Figure 6.2 shows the *value function* of the situation just described and is explained below.

Figure 6.2: prospect theory, the value function

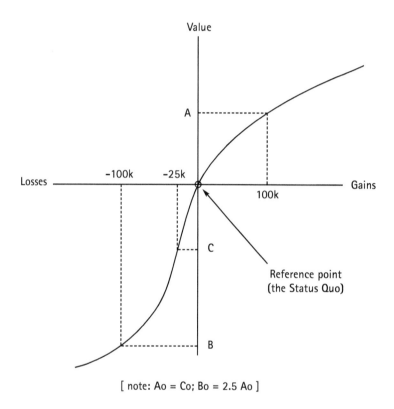

[note: Ao = Co; Bo = 2.5 Ao]

That moment in time when you're lying in bed and not risking anything and decide to tot up your wealth, coming up with a figure of a round $1 million describes your status quo. There is a feeling attached to this status quo and in prospect theory this is called the reference point. In the diagram, it is shown by the circle at the very centre.

On the value line, anything above the reference point is a positive feeling (pleasure) while anything below the reference point is a negative feeling (pain).

The horizontal line is the gains or losses line. If you move *right* from the reference point you are making a gain and if you move *left* you are making a loss.

This is the set-up when you shower and go down for breakfast. You are at the centre of the diagram, feeling secure in your status quo. Then John calls and he tells you that if you venture with him in the real estate project you stand to gain $100,000.

Immediately, you have a gut reaction, and focus on the *addition* – the *change* – in wealth and status quo involved. Your mental marker goes to the right to the point marked 100K in Figure 6.2. The pleasure value to you of this gain is at point A, shown in the diagram as reflecting off the curve.

You then discuss the downside and John tells you that potentially you also stand to lose $100,000. Your loss marker shoots to the left and you get this wrenching feeling to which you put a negative feeling at point B. You decline the offer.

Your reaction is fairly typical and logical. Point B is about two and a half times farther away from the reference point than point A. Experiments, in fact, have shown that normally a loss has about two and a half times the impact of a gain of the same size.

John then asks you what is the maximum loss you would be willing to take for a potential gain of $100,000. You figure that point C would be about as painful as point A is pleasurable and you put a figure on that of $25,000.

Looking at the situation through prospect theory, therefore, illuminates a lot of things about the seemingly straightforward conversation you had with John.

Before looking at the shape of the value function in greater detail, please note two things. The first is that in this situation you wanted a big potential gain and a small potential loss. This is one of the main reasons, in addition to the purely arithmetical ones, why in investment we must always try to keep losses small and let profits run.

Second, although not featured in the short case study, the isolation effect may come into play as well. What if John works in real estate and has always offered you business projects related to real estate. What if, this time, he came up with a manufacturing project rather than a real estate one? Although your trust in John's integrity and business acumen is unchanged, you may well view the proposed manufacturing project differently.

Or what if John told you that this time, in contrast to previous occasions, there are no tangible assets involved but only an option on a lease? Again, this might make you look at the project a different way.

The shape of the value curve

Kahneman and Tversky concluded, after years of research, that the value curve is concave for gains and convex for losses. The curve is also steeper for losses than for gains.

The top right quadrant of Figure 6.2 shows that as gains increase and move to the right, the additional value derived from the gains will increase but at an increasingly slower rate. This implies that there is risk aversion.

The shape of the value curve helps explain why, in the experxample on certain gains, people preferred the certain gain of $100 rather than taking a 50:50 risk of getting $200 or nothing. In terms of what we discussed earlier, about the foundation of finance, this implies that there was not enough motivation to attach uncertainty to capital, in this case the $100 sure gain.

On the other hand, the bottom left quadrant of Figure 6.2 is convex and indicates that as the losses increase, one feels more pain, but at a decreasing rate.

The shape of the value curve in this quadrant indicates that when making losses people tend to be risk seeking. In the experxample on facing a certain loss, for instance, people who are facing a certain loss of $100 prefer to toss a coin and then either lose $200 or, with luck, lose nothing.

It is also very important to note that the curve on the loss side of things is much steeper than on the gain side. As noted, this means losses have a much higher impact than gains, by some two and a half times. This is a manifestation of loss aversion. Losses are much more painful than gains are pleasurable and, as pleasure-seeking beings, we therefore make our best attempt to seek gains and avoid losses.

The shape of the value curve for different individuals, of course, varies. What we have examined is a generalised curve.[23] Some individuals might have quite a steep curve on the gains side meaning that gains give them a lot of pleasure, without apparently diminishing too much. Others might have a more shallow curve on the loss side, meaning they are not so loss averse or are somewhat inured to losses.

A value function is not only specific to an individual but is also tied to the reference point; the status quo the person happens to be in at a particular time. We should best think of the value function as being dynamic, changing over time. If the status quo satisfaction hypothesis I proposed is valid, the shape of the value function would change depending on the subject's satisfaction, or otherwise, with the status quo.

Entrepreneurs and speculators are likely to have a value curve quite different from someone who seeks a tranquil, secure job. Value curves might not be as smooth as suggested. Value curves are also likely to change with age and depend on the experiences a person has been through.

---

[23] There is evidence which suggests a different shape for the value curve: convex in the gains region and concave in the loss region. The original Kahneman and Tversky version discussed in the main text seems to be more in line with behaviour but as yet there is no conclusive verdict and research on this important area continues.

Professional traders

In 'Do Behavioural Biases Affect Prices?' Joshua D. Coval and Tyler Shumway report on their studies of proprietary traders on the Chicago Board of Trade. Coval and Shumway found that the traders were highly loss-averse.

Traders with morning losses were about 16% more likely to assume above-average afternoon risk than traders with morning gains. As a result, during the afternoon, losing traders chased securities to higher prices and sold securities at lower prices than those which prevailed previously. However, within ten minutes of such trades, prices reverted to their earlier levels. Short-term afternoon price volatility was found to be positively related to the prevalence of morning losses among traders, but overall afternoon price volatility was not.

Aversion and investing

Investors seek pleasure and avoid pain and their appetite for risk and uncertainty depends on their status quo and how they react to gains or losses. The value function tries to capture this reaction. Although it seems that much work still needs be done to refine our understanding, the value function is one of the most interesting insights in behavioural finance. The value function forms part of Kahneman and Tversky's Prospect Theory which deals with investors' decisions about what K&T call "risky prospects".

To many investors, ambiguity is considered a pain and securities research can be seen as one way to try and lessen the ambiguity and attempt to turn uncertainty into risk as we saw on page 84, risk and uncertainty are different. Our assessment of risk is rarely precise but the process of making the assessments adds a degree of comfort.

Investors also seek to avoid a future situation in which they regret a past decision. Regret aversion is related to loss aversion. Investors also spend a lot of time and effort struggling with the market to get even.

There are many studies on the disposition effect; that is, investors' tendency to sell winning stocks and hold on to losing stocks. Our wishful thinking that losers will turn into winners, holding on to losers to avoid admitting defeat, avoiding regret should winners turn to losers, and the buzz of raking in a profit seem to support the disposition effect.

The extent to which investors seek or avoid risk seems to be related to whether they are satisfied or not with their status quo. Investors who are not satisfied tend to seek risk while those that are satisfied with their status quo tend to want to avoid risk taking.

The certainty effect, cited in Prospect Theory, is related to "bird in the bush" behaviour. Nothing beats certainty and K&T note that people tend to underweight outcomes which are merely probable versus those that are certain – this is known as the certainty effect.

As we shall see, these concepts help explain the formation of trends and extreme prices, which are important in technical analysis.

Key concepts in this chapter

- The pleasure principle
- Aversion
- Ambiguity aversion
- Risk and uncertainty
- Regret aversion
- The reality principle
- Loss aversion
- Status quo satisfaction hypothesis
- Get-evenitis
- Disposition effect
- Prospect theory
- Certainty effect
- Isolation effect
- Value function

Chapter Seven –
Society: The Sentiment Of Crowds

"This matter of training oneself not to go with the crowd but to be able to zig when the crowd zags, in my opinion, is one of the most important fundamentals of investment success. Huge profits are frequently available to those who zig when most of the financial community is zagging, providing they have strong indications they are right in their zigging."

Philip A. Fisher, *Developing an Investment Philosophy*

"There is a tide in the affairs of men.
Which taken at the flood, leads on to fortune;
Omitted, all the voyage of their life,
Is bound in shallows and in miseries.
On such a full sea are we now afloat,
And we must take the current when it serves,
Or lose our ventures."

Julius Caesar, by William Shakespeare

What this chapter is about

The prime mover of prices in the market is sentiment. Sentiment transmits itself within the groups and crowds which make up the market.

This chapter looks at the impact of news and sentiment on the electronic crowd which makes up today's market and how we are subject to emotional contagion. The behaviour of crowds is examined via Gustave Le Bon who, a century ago, wrote one of the best empirical studies of crowd behaviour.

We next see how crowd sentiment is reflected in price graph patterns such as triangles and broadening formations.

We also look at information cascades and virtual (and vicious) spirals and conclude with George Soros' theory of reflexivity.

Anticipation and sentiment

Investment involves anticipation. We all know from experience that the sort of future we anticipate depends on our sentiment today. Webster's dictionary captures the meaning of sentiment admirably when it defines it as "an idea coloured by emotion." Note that the idea is *of the future*, but the emotion *is today's*.

What things are worth in the future depends on our sentiment today and, therefore, market sentiment – or the emotion people in the market have about the future – is what moves and determines prices.

So pervasive is sentiment, in fact, that human biologist Desmond Morris tied it to skirt hemlines as follows:

> If we look at the rise and fall of the skirt, decade by decade in the 20th century, it is clear that short skirts arrived in periods of economic buoyancy and long skirts reappeared during periods of economic decline. The short skirts of the roaring twenties were replaced by the long skirts of the depression-hit thirties; the long skirts of the austere post-war period in the late forties were replaced by the tiny miniskirts of the swinging sixties. These in turn made way for the long skirts of the seventies' recession. It is as if young females, influenced by the mood of society, revealed their level of optimism and self-confidence by the level of their hems.

It is ironic that prices, on which so much depends, are determined by fickle sentiment.

The electronic crowd

But are the participants in a market a *crowd*? When we say crowd we do not usually think of people in a market. We tend to think of a crowd as being a rather unorganised gathering of people with a rather loose sense of purpose: peace demonstrators out on the streets, triumphant soccer supporters, and such.

We do not really think of soccer supporters while in the stadium watching the game as being a disorderly crowd. Rather, at that stage, they are spectators: they are organised, and each has a seat, at least notionally. The emotion of the fans is driven by the soccer game itself, not by the crowd, though this changes when these same supporters run amok to demonstrate against an unfair referee.

People in a market, though organised, are still human beings with ideas coloured by emotion. They are susceptible to fear and greed, can feel pleasure and pain, can hope, and can decide to buy securities or dump them. And although, unlike the old days, we as investors do not usually meet physically in the marketplace, we do meet digitally at all hours in cyberspace where there are news channels, opinion pieces, forums, blogs and trading platforms. This organised – though dispersed – crowd which we call a market expresses itself every minute by buying and selling securities and we can see what the general sentiment is by simply looking at what the price is doing.

Market sentiment

Market sentiment is much like the tide in which the different securities are floating. When sentiment is healthy, good news pushes the market further up and bad news is ignored. When sentiment is poor, the market quickly reacts to any bad news and good news cannot console it.

Before one takes a position in the market, one must try and get some idea of this market tide. Is it at the ebb or at the flow? Or somewhere in between?

The impact of news

A modern market is also more than a crowd. It is part of human society with its fashions, ideas, culture and all the other factors which impinge on its attitudes and its expectations.

This means that the market is not a homogeneous mass of investors. It is heterogeneous. Different investors have different time horizons and are looking for different forces to power their investment performance. A long-term investor would be rather indifferent to day-to-day fluctuations in the market and will be looking for substantial movements over the longer term. A day trader, on the other hand, thrives on these day-to-day movements and is not really concerned with longer-term forces except in so far as he or she can link them to short-term fluctuations.

This implies that the main mover of markets – news – impacts the different components of the market to different degrees and in different ways. The impact primarily depends on the relevance of the news to the market movements which the investor is observing. A long-term investor, for example, is sensitive to news which has a long-term significance and tends to ignore news of a temporary nature. A long-term investor is not likely to pay too much attention to the fact that an important internet merchant had its website down for two hours but, for a short-term investor, this is likely to signal a short-term fall in the stock price and the stock is shorted forthwith.[24]

Tide and tempo

An extension of this observation is that, because markets are heterogeneous, they do not share the same tempo. This observation comes out clearly in the previous example: the short-term investor acts immediately while the long-term investor investigates and will act, if appropriate, in due course.

News travels through a market at a somewhat measured pace, even in this electronic age of instant communication.[25]

Many people starting on their study of investments think that investing is about number crunching and esoteric models. These are indeed important tools – they help bring objectivity to an economic situation by suspending our emotions – but, fundamentally, investing is about the anticipations made by markets, and markets are part of society.

Emotional contagion

What turns a number of individuals into a crowd is emotional contagion, because an individual in a crowd feels and expresses the same emotions as the rest of the crowd. The individual can feel the same anger, fear, hope and greed which has taken hold of those around him or her.

---

[24] This observation has to be qualified somewhat: the long-term investor is likely to ignore such downtime unless it signals something of deeper significance, e.g. security risks or lax management. Such incidents should therefore still be investigated by the long-term investor.

[25] There is also the natural tendency for some people to react faster than others, either because they understand things quicker, or presume they do, or because they are more impulsive.

The emotional contagion in the groups and crowds which make up the market is one of the reasons why investors tend to herd and copy each others' actions and thus form trends.

The communication between individuals can be verbal or non-verbal, such as body posture. We often do the same as others are doing without realising it. Research has shown that the premotor cortex and parietal areas of our brain are activated when we mimic others. The premotor cortex is the outer layer of the brain on top of the head just behind the forehead while the parietal area lies behind this, like a band from ear to ear.

Recently, during experiments using macaque monkeys, it was discovered that our brain contains widely dispersed mirror neurons which are sensitive to the movement, emotion and intention of the persons around us. What we sense is then replicated within ourselves by activation of our own brain. This brain-to-brain link has long been suspected but pin-pointed only recently. It accounts for our taking something of the accent of those around us and how modes of behaviour tend to transmit themselves from person to person.

In my years working as an investment adviser I had the opportunity to meet many couples and I was always impressed by how husband and wife, over the years, developed the same attitude, approach and even mannerisms.

Indeed, psychologists found that hearing the same person express the same opinion multiple times had nearly the same effect on the listener as hearing an opinion from a number of people. This applies to all sorts of opinions, from financial opinions to concerns about terrorism.

Researchers are doing quite a lot of work on social contagion and empathy and are making very interesting discoveries.

Along with the premotor cortex and parietal areas, the amygdala, which we mentioned in chapter Two, also seems to play a part. The amygdala has a role in empathy and emotional atonement and thus makes emotional contagion possible.

Group culture

Groups have their own culture. A group's culture, rituals, symbols and ways of doing things come into sharp contrast when an outsider enters a group – both for the group and the individual concerned. This happens, for example, when we change jobs and come face-to-face with another company's culture. Successful companies usually have very strong cultures and newcomers either adapt or are made to leave.

Group culture gives coherence to a group and makes teamwork easier because team members know where the other person is coming from and members are all reading from the same page. The newcomer is told: "This is the way we do things around here." The individual, for their part, can hang responsibility for certain decisions on the group and group culture often supports relationships between people who fit in. On the other hand, *groupthink* may be so strong as to cause even intelligent and otherwise strong-willed people to make stupid mistakes.

Financial firms throughout the world tend to have strong cultures and symbols. Perhaps this is because, like an army, financial firms are battling against the uncertainties of the market and so need strong group coherence.

Gustave's crowd

Gustave Le Bon was born in 1841 in Nogent-le-Retrou in France. At first, after medical studies, he practised medicine in Paris but being of an intensely inquisitive mind he later travelled throughout Europe, Asia and North Africa. He wrote on anthropology, sociology and physics.

He achieved fame when in 1895 he published his book, *Psychologie des foules*, translated as *The Crowd*, and sometimes sub-titled as 'A Study of the Popular Mind'. This book was a bestseller and very influential – it is said to have influenced Adolf Hitler's propaganda techniques in *Mein Kampf* which, if true, shows both its effectiveness and the double-edged nature of its ideas and insights. *The Crowd* is a great read to this day and in it Le Bon shares many observations about crowd behaviour in a percipient and lively manner.

Le Bon suggests that the individual in the crowd – wherever that crowd may be – is likely to lose his critical faculties and to get carried away by the emotion of the crowd, even if this leads to primitive and barbaric behaviour. While in a crowd, the individual is easily carried away and convinced, and the crowd's emotional contagion makes it possible for leaders to manipulate it.

In what follows, I will focus on aspects of the book which seem relevant to markets and crowds, but there are many other passages in the book which give the reader great insight into crowd behaviour and these might also prove to be helpful when trying to guess where a market is likely to head.[26]

Le Bon starts off by examining the general characteristics of the crowd and notes in the introduction that "men never shape their conduct upon the teaching of pure reason." He goes to the point on the first page of Chapter 1 and states:

> Under certain given circumstances, and only under those circumstances, an agglomeration of men presents new characteristics very different from those of the individuals composing it. The sentiments and ideas of all the persons in the gathering

---

[26] *The Crowd* and other books by Le Bon are available from various sites on the internet for free download.

take one and the same direction, and their conscious personality vanishes. A collective mind is formed, doubtless transitory, but presenting very clearly defined characteristics. The gathering has thus become what, in the absence of a better expression, I will call an organised crowd, or, if the term is considered preferable, a psychological crowd. It forms a single being, and is subjected to the *law of the mental unity of crowds*.

In a crowd every sentiment and act is contagious, and contagious to such a degree that an individual readily sacrifices his personal interest to the collective interest. This is an aptitude very contrary to his nature, and of which a man is scarcely capable, except when he makes part of a crowd.

Importantly, from our point of view, dealing with markets which are often widespread but linked electronically, a crowd need not be gathered in the same place. Le Bon notes that "the primary characteristics of a crowd about to become organised, do not always involve the simultaneous presence of a number of individuals on one spot."

Le Bon emphasised that the character of crowds is emotional, rapidly formed and short of duration. We see this in modern markets all the time – the rapid, full-scale selling in time of national calamities and the wave upon wave of buying when greed grips the market and an asset class seems to acquire the Midas touch.

Part of the reason for the crowd's tumultuous actions comes from the fact that it is not driven by logic, but instead they seem to be only capable of "simple and extreme sentiments".

This helps explain why certain simple concepts – some based on analysis, some on mere impressions – often take hold of a market and seem to dominate it: The Nifty Fifty, Irrational Exuberance, The New Economy, Productivity, the Commodities Boom, EBITDA, Tech, TMT (technology, media, telecommunications sector), BRIC (Brazil, Russia, India, China).

The concepts these words and acronyms refer to have made and lost people a lot of money. When you hear something of this ilk repeatedly, be sceptical, and examine the hard evidence. Then play along with the crowd, or be a contrarian, as appropriate. (We will examine how such concepts feed on each other and move markets later on in this Chapter when I deal with Soros's reflectivity principle.)

As Le Bon states that the ideas suggested to crowds can only be effective if they take "a very absolute, uncompromising and simple shape" and in the "guise of images".

BRIC, for example, is a simple idea. All four countries are currently developing rapidly and represent the largest of the emerging markets. However, the BRIC concept lumps the countries into one big bucket even though the circumstances of each country are peculiar to each. Be all this as it may, BRIC is a convenient label for a mutual fund and the financial industry therefore gladly adopted the acronym.

BRIC, of course, is nearly identical to brick, with its associations of being a basic building block, and durable, and is a very easy word to remember.

Le Bon notes how crowds often reason by lumping together dissimilar things which are only tenuously related. Crowds often go from particular cases to great generalisations. According to Le Bon: "Words whose sense is the most ill-defined are sometimes those that possess the most influence." Certain vague words – such as democracy, socialism, and liberty – are often accorded "truly magical power".

Seneca and the crowd

"You ask me to say what you should consider it particularly important to avoid. My answer is this: a mass crowd. It is something to which you cannot entrust yourself yet without risk. I at any rate am ready to confess my own frailty in this respect. I never come back home with quite the same moral character I went out with; something or other becomes unsettled where I had achieved internal peace, some one or other of the things I had put to flight reappears on the scene. Associating with people in large numbers is actually harmful: there is not one of them that will not make some vice or other attractive to us. And inevitably enough, the larger the size of the crowd we mingle with, the greater the danger."

Seneca 'Letters from a Stoic' (Letter VII)

Triangles and broadening formations

The footprints of the emotions which grip crowds and markets can often be seen in so-called ascending or descending triangles and broadening formations.

If one goes on any website which shows stock price graphs and calls up three or four stocks and then checks the price pattern over a number of years, one would notice that there comes a period during any stock's life, sometimes lasting months, when the stock basically goes nowhere and the price simply coils around itself. We say the stock is range bound, held within two prices; the price seems to be moving within a *rectangle*, which is what this price formation is called.

On closer observation one usually detects a slight incline or decline in the range of prices jailing the stock and this usually gives a hint as to the direction the stock will eventually take when it breaks out of the range. Sometimes, as time goes by, the range even closes further, so that a *triangle* is formed.

The triangle can be either descending (with successive lower highs), such as that shown in Figure 7.1, or ascending (with successive higher lows), as shown in Figure 7.2. Generally, descending triangles are bearish while ascending triangles are bullish.[27] These price formations indicate that the stock is consolidating its energy and the longer it is held captive within the range, the sharper and bigger a breakout is likely to be. Sometimes, instead of getting narrower, a range actually gets wider, in what is called a broadening formation, as shown in Figure 7.3. This is quite a rare formation.

Figure 7.1: a descending triangle with successive lower highs

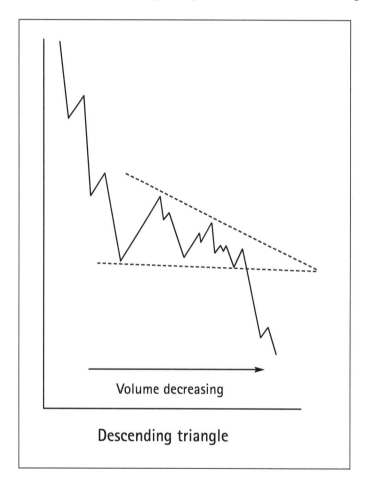

Volume decreasing

Descending triangle

---

[27] A triangle can also be symmetrical, formed by waves of declining amplitude, and this is generally a continuation pattern, that is, the previous trend is likely to continue.

Figure 7.2: an ascending triangle with successive higher lows

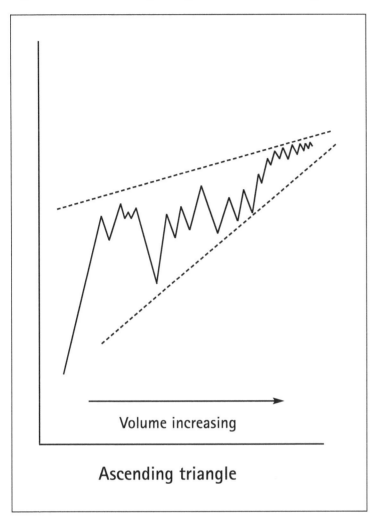

Volume increasing

Ascending triangle

Figure 7.3: a broadening formation with a progressively wider range

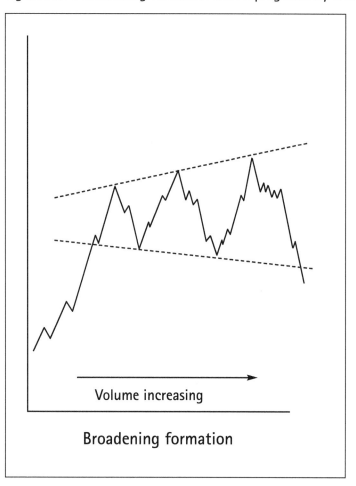

Volume increasing

Broadening formation

John Murphy, in *Technical Analysis of the Financial Markets*, states that this formation "represents a market that is out of control and unusually emotional. Because this pattern also represents an unusual amount of public participation, it most often occurs at major market tops – a bearish formation."

While a triangle is accompanied by decreasing volume (but a high volume on the breakout), in a broadening formation volume is increasing, in conformity with wide participation.

Robert Edwards and John Magee, in their *Technical Analysis of Stock Trends*, describe the three patterns discussed as follows:

> If the symmetrical triangle presents a picture of doubt awaiting clarification, and the rectangle a picture of controlled conflict, the broadening formation may be said to suggest a market lacking intelligent sponsorship and out of control – a situation,

usually, in which the public is excitedly committed and which is being whipped around by wild rumours.[28]

Emotion in the market and the pull and push of different opinions – which usually filter themselves into two broad groups – can often be detected on stock graphs by increased volatility and huge swings. The specific biases at play are much like those discussed in support and resistance trading ranges, only stronger.

Crowds are not always wrong

Various authors have shown that, in certain circumstances, crowds can be much smarter than an individual thinking alone. Scott Page, for example, contends that a crowd can indeed be smart if it is composed of individuals who have diverse cognitive skills, if the information within the crowd can be aggregated and if the right incentives are in place. The individuals making up the crowd, after all, must have diverse outlooks and cognitive capacities in the way they understand and interpret situations, their heuristics, and how they go about predicting events.

The information from the individuals forming the crowd must be aggregated and analysed, in the same way that the crowd of participants on a stock exchange act through that one place or how citizens express themselves in a democracy by voting freely at the same time.

The third essential element is that the individuals in the crowd must be suitably incentivised so that they make an effort to be right and try to avoid being wrong. In other words, there should be some sort of consequence for their being right or wrong.

Under these circumstances it seems that a crowd beats an individual in certain kinds of problems. For example, a group of people is more likely to guess the number of jelly beans in a jar than an individual. A collective effort is also likely to better guess the winners of Academy Awards. When facing difficult questions, it has been shown that even if only a small number of individuals in the group know the correct answer, the group is likely to beat individuals who are expert in the field.

Howard Rheingold takes a slightly different approach and shows how co-operation between individuals not only leads to solutions otherwise unavailable but is one of the conditions for human progress.[29]

---

[28] Robert Edwards and John Magee, *Technical Analysis of Stock Trends*, 8th edition, p.148.

[29] For an interesting talk on this subject by Rheingold, visit www.ted.com. TED (Technology, Education, Design) is a forum for foremost thinkers to speak about innovation and inspiration and to disseminate great ideas. TED started in 1984 and is owned by the private non-profit Sapling Foundation.

Information cascades

In the first part of this chapter we saw how sentiment plays an essential role in the valuation of securities because the market, being a dispersed crowd, is emotional and it is the market which ultimately grants or withdraws value from a security, depending on how it is anticipating the future. We saw that it is important to ascertain market sentiment and come to an opinion of whether it is right or wrong. We then saw how emotion travels within the members of a crowd or organisation via emotional contagion, which leads to group coherence.

By looking at the work of Le Bon we got an idea of how crowds behave and we then saw peculiar price graph formations which an emotionally charged market is likely to leave in its wake. We noted, then, that crowds are not always dumb but can sometimes be surprisingly smart.

All of this comes together in information cascades. An information cascade can be compared to a market avalanche. In an avalanche, a mass of snow in the mountains breaks off from the rest and starts rolling and sliding down the slopes. The large mass of snow gathers pace and even more mass and momentum as it rushes down the slopes of the mountain, becoming a great force.

Market avalanche

A similar phenomenon takes place in markets. Markets go to extremes, both up and down. The momentum of the market takes-over investors and there is a rush to the top followed by a sharp, frantic rush to the bottom.

In every case of a market avalanche, though, we start off with a spark of information. The information can be endogenous, coming from the financial market itself, or the information can be exogenous, coming from the general economy.

An example of an exogenous information spark would be a sharp and unexpected increase in the consumer price index, used to measure inflation. This might be taken to mean much higher inflation to come, with concomitant increases in interest rates. If the market expects interest rates to rise, future company cash flows would be discounted at a higher rate and stock valuations would fall. Expected inflation can therefore lead to a sharp correction in market levels. Depending on the state of the market, this information spark can itself then gather a following and there is reinforcement of this information as stock prices actually start to fall.

A market avalanche can start off with an exogenous spark and continue with endogenous ones, as in this last example. Sometimes, it is the other way round: the market starts falling, giving off an endogenous information spark which gathers pace and leads to a recession, an exogenous stimulus, as the lower stock prices lead to lower consumption and investment.

Keep in mind in all this that the economy is one dynamic whole and one should never over-compartmentalise its workings.

Information feeds on itself and has real world effects. In the recent commodities boom, for example, we saw commodity prices rising both because a number of countries with huge populations were developing their economies rapidly and also because investors invested increasing portions of their funds in commodities as prices rose. Seeing this, investment product providers gave the market the instruments it needed, such as commodity exchange traded funds (ETFs).

A virtuous spiral is thus formed from such positive feedback loops, and equally a vicious spiral can be caused by negative feedback loops.

Spiralling beliefs

Notice that in an information cascade leading to a bullish or bearish spiral, individuals put aside the private information they have – securities analysis, opinion, etc – and adopt the market crowds' beliefs and opinions, in a way similar to Le Bon's description: "The sentiments and ideas of all the persons in the gathering take one and the same direction, and their conscious personality vanishes."

Of course, market observers know that there are many information sparks which die quickly and never take off. These are happening all the time. The market nearly always consists of waves within waves, very rarely in a straight line.

When the market is going sideways there are many such short-lived information sparks contradicting each other and leaving the market trading within a range. At some point, though, you get a powerful piece of information which leads the market in one direction or the other, overcoming all opposition, or else you get many pieces of information at the same time all pointing one way, such as is common during results seasons when many companies are reporting at the same time (usually in April, July, October and January for companies with a normal January to December fiscal year).

Investors always have a scenario in mind and information serves to confirm or contradict that scenario. The longer the directionless period, the more anxious investors are to have their scenarios confirmed or denied.

Information cascades have three interesting aspects:

1. They show market crowd behaviour at its best (or worst) and are purely a crowd phenomenon.

2. At the very least, the initial market direction taken during information cascades is often right.

3. They often lead to overshooting and extremes which can give alert investors great entry points.

In the next section we look at how George Soros, the billionaire investor, used information cascades within his theory of reflexivity.

Soros and reflexivity

In his theory of reflexivity George Soros suggests an analytical framework to help us understand market dynamics.[30] Soros contends that disequilibrium occurs because the market departs from fundamentals and is taken over by participants' perceptions as well as the information content of the price movement itself.[31]

Soros uses *reflexivity* in two senses. In the first, it describes structures, such as markets, which involve thinking participants. In the second sense, he uses the term to describe instances where feedback disrupts both the events themselves and the way participants perceive them. This leads to a disequilibrium in the market.

He notes that "reflexive processes that become historically significant tend to follow an initially self-reinforcing, but eventually self-defeating, pattern. That is what I call the boom/bust sequence."[32]

Soros believes that three processes are at work in a reflexive system:

1. There is the underlying trend, which in a market influences prices.
2. There is the prevailing bias, which is how participants perceive a market.
3. There are the securities' prices themselves, which are determined by the other two factors but which, at a point, can themselves influence the underlying trend and the prevailing bias, via two-way feedback.

A process is set in motion which goes from equilibrium to disequilibrium and from boom to bust and this process provides the acute observer great opportunities.

The process unfolds as follows: At first, a trend is not recognised for what it is but eventually it is recognised and this recognition brings with it reinforcement. In this *initial phase*, the prevailing trend and the prevailing bias support each other.

As things develop, the bias becomes increasingly exaggerated and divorced from the fundamentals. The bias may be tested by shocks to the system but the more shocks

---

[30] The description of the theory which follows is principally based on Soros' writings in the two books referenced. Soros' ideas keep evolving, albeit within the general reflexivity framework set out in these two books.

[31] In later writings and speeches, Soros points out that markets are never really in equilibrium and that we use the concept of equilibrium to try and understand market behaviour.

[32] George Soros, *Soros on Soros*.

the bias withstands, the stronger it becomes. In this *period of acceleration* the bias takes stronger hold of the market (or other reflexive system).

Eventually, participants themselves recognise their own bias, belief subsides, doubt grows and after this *moment of truth* there comes stagnation, or a *twilight period*.

As belief subsides, the trend will reverse at the *crossover point*. An opposite trend develops and a bias in the opposite direction is created and this causes the acceleration of the old trend that qualifies as a *crash*.

In Figure 7.4, I suggest a depiction of the process described in the theory of reflexivity.

Figure 7.4: Reflexivity

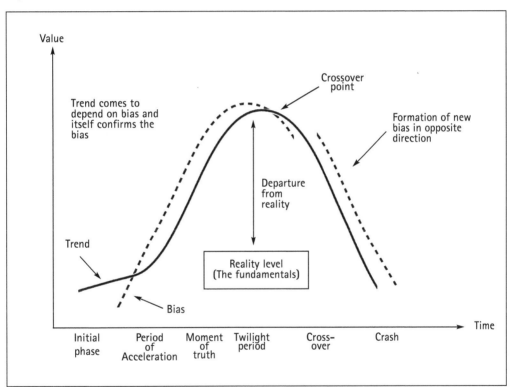

Soros gives practical examples of this theory, explaining, for example, the conglomerate boom of the late 1960s. He insists, however, that the origin of his theory was philosophical and abstract at first, and he only realised its practical significance, and its market applications, as time went by and his ideas developed and became clearer. In fact, he very enthusiastically applies the theory to societies and regimes, such as the Soviet Union, and to other historical processes, showing how societies too go from boom to bust.

Soros' thinking is based on the observation that due to the complexity of the real world, and due to the fact that our actions themselves influence what we observe, it is impossible for us to know what exists. Our knowledge of reality is defective. Other participants in the market have the same problem. At any one time, therefore, either or both the market and ourselves can be right or wrong. One should continually observe and test what one is thinking about the state of the market and what the state of the market is implying.

Soros' reflexivity provides a philosophical model which illustrates how price and market behaviour are intimately bound with participants' thought and emotional processes.

Society, crowds and investing

- Emotional contagion and mirroring are a part of every human group and these phenomena help spread sentiment through markets. Sentiment is the main determinant of price in the short-term and, even though markets are heterogeneous, with different people having different objectives and investment horizons, trends form and prices often go to extremes. The dynamics are captured by Soros' reflexivity principle.

- Participants in financial markets can be seen as being part of a crowd, often connected together electronically over the internet and on electronic exchanges. Markets, like crowds, are susceptible to herding and the effects of information cascades forming virtuous (or vicious) spirals.

- Technical analysis captures extreme emotion in markets when it describes triangles and broadening formations.

Key concepts in this chapter

- Sentiment
- Heterogeneity of markets
- News
- Emotional contagion
- Mirror neurons
- Triangles and broadening formations
- Information cascade
- Endogenous and exogenous information
- Virtuous (vicious) spiral
- Reflexivity

Chapter Eight – Gender

"Was this the face that launch'd a thousand ships,
And burnt the topless towers of Ilium?
Sweet Helen, make me immortal with a kiss."

Christopher Marlowe's *Doctor Faustus*, referring to Helen of Troy

What this chapter is about

We start by looking at two scientific studies that have investigated whether men and women can be induced to discount the future more heavily and take greater risks. This will help us to understand how men and women evaluate investment decisions differently. We then examine the effects of the hormones testosterone and cortisol on risk taking.

The ultimatum game – in which one offers a piece of the pie to another in a win-all, lose-all situation – reveals interesting aspects of human behaviour. We also take a look at the brain's sense of fairness.

We end with a discussion of the differences in male and female attitudes to risk.

External stimuli on the personal discount rate

Investment can be seen as a bridge in time between what we have to spend today and what we can expect to receive at some point in time in the future. We have seen that this expectation of future reward is coloured by sentiment – how we are feeling about ourselves and the world around us and by how we see the future.

This chapter describes a series of experiments which show that the discount factor we use – that is, by how much we discount the future – depends on various motivational stimuli we have been subjected to, including pretty faces.

Men induced to discount the future more heavily

Margo Wilson and Martin Daly, psychologists at McMaster University in Hamilton, Ontario, asked themselves a piquant question: do stimuli which induce a mating opportunity mindset bring about a higher personal discount rate? The participants were asked to look at pictures of the opposite sex and at pictures of cars.

Wilson and Daly conducted the experiment on 96 male and 113 female undergraduates who volunteered for a study of 'preferences for things we like' as part of a psychology course. After placing the students in different groups, to ensure proper experimental design, Wilson and Daly then measured each student's discount factor to determine at what point they would forgo an immediate monetary reward for a bigger one in the future. Then, depending on the group they were in, they were shown 12 pictures of 'hot' and 'not hot' members of the opposite sex, and pictures of 'hot' and 'not hot' cars. Wilson and Daly then measured the discount factor a second time to see whether these images had any effect.

According to the authors, "as predicted, discounting increased significantly in men who viewed attractive women, but not in men who viewed unattractive women or women who viewed men." The authors also found that hot cars had no significant effect on either men or women.

Wilson and Daly's work is interesting because they demonstrated how the discount rate is susceptible to experimental manipulation by inducing a mating opportunity mindset in their subjects.

Prior to this experiment it was already known that the discount rate varied with personality. Heroin addicts, for example, were found to have a higher discount rate than members of a control group and, furthermore, an addict's discount rate increased with the delay since their last injection. It was also known that men discount the future more steeply than women. Somehow, with men, this steep discounting tends to carry over to monetary matters, thus men's generally more risk-taking nature.

Researchers discovered from functional Magnetic Resonance Imaging (fMRI) studies that when young, heterosexual males passively view beautiful female faces there is an activation of a reward circuitry in the brain, particularly the nucleus accumbens, which we discussed earlier as the part of the brain responsible for assessing risk and reward. Furthermore, the anticipation of money and its actual receipt also stimulated a set of reward regions in the brain.

Inducing greater risk taking

If attractive females can make men discount the future more steeply, can they also induce them to take bigger risks?

In one experiment, by Brian Knutson of Stanford University and his team, the subjects were 15 heterosexual men who were shown three types of images: positive (couples in erotic poses), negative (snakes or spiders), and neutral (household appliances). They were subsequently asked to bet either $1 or $0.10. They had equal chances of winning or losing and were entitled to collect any winnings.

The researchers found that the erotic images produced many more $1 bets than the negative or neutral images. During the experiment, the men were monitored via fMRI scanners and the researchers noticed that activity in the brain's nucleus accumbens spontaneously increases before financial risk taking.

It seems, therefore, that when the brain's nucleus accumbens and other reward-associated areas are stimulated males are apt to more steeply discount the future and to take higher risks.

Other researchers have studied the hormone testosterone.

Hormones and risk taking

Testosterone is a steroid hormone produced in the testes in males and in the ovaries in females. It is normally associated with the male gender because an adult male body produces about fifty times more testosterone than a female body, though females are very sensitive to the hormone.

Testosterone plays a major role in sexual functions by enhancing libido and energy, but it also has a role in the production of red blood cells and in protecting the body against osteoporosis. The level of testosterone in the body, both male and female, varies widely such that a high-testosterone woman can actually have more of the hormone than a low-testosterone male. The level of testosterone in a person can be measured through saliva tests.

Testosterone and trading

John Coates and Joe Herbert of Cambridge University investigated the effect of testosterone on male traders at an unnamed City of London bank over eight consecutive business days. Coates himself was a trader on Wall Street before he went into academia.

Coates and Herbert tested the saliva of male traders in the morning and in the afternoon, before and after the bulk of trading for the day. They found that the level of testosterone was directly related to their profitability during the day. Not only was a higher morning testosterone level associated with higher profits during the day, but the success achieved raised levels even further, leading to even higher confidence and risk-taking.

One trader, for example, who one day made profits several times his daily average, saw his testosterone level shoot up by 56% of this average for the other days. Another trader, after a six-day winning streak, with twice the average daily profit, had testosterone 74% above mean levels.

This sort of behaviour, of course, is great in a rising market because the winner effect leads to higher exposure and everyone is a genius in a bull market. At times when the markets are not so directional, however, the higher risk taking may backfire, leading to heavy losses.

The researchers noted that since hormones have cognitive and behavioural effects, an elevated level of steroids during periods of high market volatility "may shift risk preferences and even affect a trader's ability to engage in rational choice." They also note that one of their reviewers had suggested "that these steroid-feedback loops may be relevant to explaining why market volatility tends to come in waves, a phenomenon economists term autoregressive conditional heteroskedasticity (ARCH)."

This wave pattern of prices and volatility is ubiquitous on price graphs and is a reflection of human behaviour in markets. Coates and Herbert's study suggests an explanation which ties our observations more deeply into the physiology of the human body.

The stress hormone – cortisol

Another hormone investigated in the Cambridge study was cortisol. Cortisol is produced in the adrenal gland and is referred to as the stress hormone. Cortisol is involved in our reaction to stress and its effects include increasing blood pressure and sugar levels.

The level of cortisol in humans varies very widely. Day-to-day, the level of cortisol varies even more than does the level of testosterone. Cortisol levels, however, seem to follow a broad daily cycle, being high early in the morning, presumably to prepare the body for the stress of waking up, and very low in the middle of the night, four hours or so after one goes to sleep, when sleep is at its deepest.

In many ways, cortisol has an opposite effect to testosterone in that it dampens down aggression and hyperactivity. Cortisol leads to risk aversion and is likely to rise when the market is weak and prices are falling. High levels of cortisol flowing in the veins of market participants, therefore, could have the effect of pushing the market down.

Coates and Herbert found that "a trader's cortisol rises with both the variance of his trading and the volatility of the market." So here there are two factors at play: trading results affect the level of cortisol and choppy markets induce a higher level of the stress hormone.

The findings suggest testosterone can lead to bubbles, while cortisol may have an influence in market crashes.

Hormone levels, therefore, tend to affect trading behaviour and also go higher or lower in response to market conditions, helping to create a market's directional and directionless movements.

Sensing this, traders are said to take or be given hormone supplements to speed up or dampen their trading enthusiasm.

The ultimatum game

Suppose you volunteer to participate in a psychology experiment and you are seated in a small room being briefed about what's about to happen. The researcher tells you that in another room in the building there is another person being briefed about the same experiment. Like you, the other person knows you exist but not who you are, nor whether you are male or female, young or old. The researcher tells you that you are going to be given $100 and you have to share the money with the other person. If the other person accepts what you give him or her, then you both get to keep the respective share of the pot. But if the other person refuses what you offer, then neither you nor the other person gets any money. The more you offer of the $100, the more likely it is that the other person accepts.

As always, deciding what is best is a game of logic but, being human, our behaviour nearly always becomes entangled in emotional issues. If the person in the other room was entirely logical he would accept whatever you offered, even if it was a few cents, because he knew that refusal would mean getting nothing. But such experiments involving humans report many refusals. Often, when the sum offered is too small, the person in the other room would refuse your offer outright even though the other person knows he or she would, as a result of the refusal, be getting nothing. The other person would refuse just so you suffer the consequences of your meanness.

The person offering a proportion of the money is called the proposer, and the person being offered the money is called the responder.

The game across the world

The ultimatum game has been conducted by many researchers across the world and subjected to meta-analysis, a statistical technique which combines the research conclusions of studies testing a set of related hypotheses. In one study, by Oosterbeek et al, it was found that on average proposers offered 40% of the pie. The bigger the pie, the lesser the average share they offered. The more inexperienced the proposers, the more they offered. On average, 16% of the offers were rejected. The larger the pies and the larger the offers, the lower were the rejections. If any sort of strategy is employed – strategies are allowed in certain experiments – responders would be less willing to accept what is offered. Across geographical regions, no meaningful differences in the behaviour of proposers is detected but the behaviour of responders varies.

Some of the cultural differences come as a big surprise. Amongst the Au and Gnau of Papua New Guinea, offers were often higher than 50% and, still, most of these offers were rejected.

The evidence from the wide cross-cultural studies of the ultimatum game suggest that while most financial markets across the world share the same characteristics, there can often be significant differences.

Emotional brain

There is another part of the brain which seems to play a major role in decisions of all kinds where emotions are somehow involved: the *insula*, part of the cerebral cortex, the 'grey matter' outermost layer of the brain. Knutson and Kuhnen found that risk aversion and riskless choice seems to be related to activity in this part of the brain.

fMRI scanning of proposers and responders playing the ultimatum game found that small offers and their rejection were often associated with activity in the bilateral anterior insula areas of the brain. These areas are not part of the *thinking* part of the brain, the prefrontal cortex, which is so dominant in logical persons. The left and right anterior insula areas of the brain, rather, are associated with anger, pain, distress, disgust, hunger, thirst, autonomic arousal and negative emotions. These areas of the brain have now been linked to emotions and questions of moral choice (see 'The brain's sense of fairness' below).

In his book *Mean Markets and Lizard Brains* author Terry Burnham, discussing the ultimatum game experiments, makes reference to his findings that men who reject small offers in ultimatum games have much higher levels of testosterone than those who accept. Testosterone, again, seems to be playing a significant role here.

Burnham suggests that the noted pattern of rejection might be related to the role testosterone plays in the maintenance of dominance hierarchies where socially dominant males enter into conflict situations in order to preserve their status. It seems that testosterone might be stimulating the older, more primitive parts of the brain leading to confrontation. As we saw, rejection of offers is not the logical choice.

The brain's sense of fairness

If you thought that the sense of fairness and good moral choice is a recent development of the human brain, along with co-ordination and logic, you were mistaken.

In one experiment, by Hsu et al, 26 adults were asked to make decisions about how to allocate meals to orphans. From brain imaging studies, it emerged that the stronger the activity in the insula areas of the brain, the more likely the adults spread the meals fairly.

The authors studied distributive justice, which deals with how benefits and burdens are distributed in a just and moral manner, bringing into play the trade-off between equity and efficiency.

Certain areas of the brain respond to efficiency concerns whereas the insula reacts to inequity. A third area of the brain (the caudate/septal subgenual region) synthesises a measure of utility, a unified measure of efficiency and inequity. The drive for fairness is the insula's reaction.

The authors contended that a sense of fairness is fundamental to distributive justice but the processing involved is emotional. They stated: "More generally, emotional responses related to norm violations may underlie individual differences in equity considerations and adherence to ethical rules."

This interesting and important study by Hsu, Anen and Quartz not only throws light on why responders in ultimatum games sometimes reject offers – due to what they feel is an assault on their sense of fairness – but also why markets and sports thrive when there is a sense of fairness and the absence of corruption; thus the great efforts of regulators to ensure a level playing field, and eradicate such practices as insider trading.

Lack of fairness and morals triggers a reaction by the insula and puts off participants. High testosterone individuals would prefer to die of hunger than be victimised.

Male and female attitudes to risk

Brad Barber and Terrance Odean, working at the University of California at Davis, managed to persuade an unnamed large discount broker to provide them with confidential access to the accounts of some 78,000 households which they then subjected to thorough analysis. Access to these accounts provided the researchers with a range of "natural experiments", as they describe them at one point. One study, published in 2001, commonly referred to as the "Boys will be Boys" study, dealt specifically with gender.

As we have seen earlier in this book, people tend to overestimate their knowledge and this implies that, for the same degree of risk aversion, overconfident investors tend to hold riskier portfolios, including portfolios which are under-diversified.

In previous work, Barber and Odean had shown that frequent trading tends to make performance suffer compared to benchmarks. Frequent trading seemed to be linked to overconfidence. Furthermore, the authors noted that it was difficult to explain previous findings that investors tended to act on too little information unless you bring overconfidence into the picture. Overconfidence, therefore, was a plausible explanation for frequent trading, risk seeking, and rather hasty investment decisions. Certainly, these observations were not consistent with rational behaviour.

Researchers had shown that while both men and women, exhibit overconfidence, men are generally more overconfident than women especially when it comes to undertakings which are perceived to fall in the masculine domain. Men tend to think they are more competent than women in financial matters. The research also found that the self-attribution bias in men is stronger than it is in women – that is, men had a greater tendency to attribute good performance to their own ability and this served as more fodder to the already pronounced overconfidence.

Previous studies[33] had also shown that men spent more time and money on security analysis, relied less on brokers, transacted more, expected higher returns and believed returns were more predictable, than women did. To clarify the situation: both men and women expect their portfolios to outperform the market, but men expect to outperform by a greater margin than do women.

All these findings, inevitably, indicated that men were more overconfident than women and, therefore, Barber and Odean partitioned their data on the basis of gender; the more overconfident gentlemen versus the less overconfident ladies.

After analysing the data of some 38,000 households where they could identify the gender of the person opening the account, for the six years from February 1991 to January 1997, they presented their findings:

> Consistent with the predictions of the overconfidence models, we find that the average turnover rate of common stocks for men is nearly one-and-a-half times that for women. While both men and women reduce their net returns through trading, men do so by 0.94 percentage points more a year than do women.

> The differences in turnover and return performance are even more pronounced between single men and single women. Single men trade 67 percent more than single women, thereby reducing their returns by 1.44 percentage points per year more than do single women.

While individuals, of course, vary – there are many cautious men and adventurous ladies – the "Boys will be Boys" study does indicate certain general characteristics of the two genders and perhaps suggests that men should be more cautious and ladies more aggressive.

---

[33] A summary of the research findings and the relevant references can be found in the Barber and Odean paper.

Gender and technical analysis

Gender influences the way we trade and this chapter looked at various physiological aspects which influence risk taking and the personal discount rate. While males can perhaps improve their performance by deliberately being more cautious and females by being more adventurous, the influences that make us seek risk or avoid it are often physiological.

The ultimatum game highlights the fact that emotions play a role in our decision making and it also suggests that there are subtle cultural differences from one market to another around the world.

If gender plays such an important role in risk-taking, the important role of analysis – be it fundamental, technical or quantitative – comes to the fore. All three forms of analysis, while still subjective and dependent on wise judgement, introduce measures of objectivity into the investment process with the aim that this objectivity will enhance investment performance and subdue impulses to trade and invest according to our emotional reactions.

In a sense, technical analysis is itself a heuristic which captures and simplifies market movements resulting from sentiment, emotion and prior price movements. On the basis of this users decide whether to invest or not. Technical analysis, while imperfect like all heuristics, still adds a good measure of objectivity, especially when it is scientifically based. This objectivity helps guard against reaction produced by emotion and hormones.

Key concepts in this chapter

- Discounting the future

- Personal discount rate

- Testosterone

- Cortisol

- Ultimatum game

- The insula part of the brain

PART THREE –

BEHAVIOURAL FINANCE AND TECHNICAL ANALYSIS

Chapter Nine –
Behavioural Aspects Of Technical Analysis

"All movements go too far."

Bertrand Russell

What this chapter is about

In this chapter, we first take a step back from behavioural finance to have a general look at the bare-bones essentials of the market. First, each and every transaction has three elements: *money, time, and probability*. This is the MTP framework, which is helpful in analysing not only investment decisions but also personal choices.

Second, I look at how the price of assets is formed not by economic factors alone, as most of classical finance assumes, but also by sentiment and price action, thus introducing SEP (sentiment, economics and price action) sets. Third, I introduce the *market matrix*; I see the market as consisting of trend followers, contrarians and undecided investors, some participating and others not.

In the second part of this chapter we look at how trends develop. Trends bring with them extreme price levels and support and resistance areas. Trends, extreme prices and support and resistance all provide the investor with opportunities for high probability trades.

The dynamics of technical analysis can be seen as a struggle between trend followers, contrarians and the undecided (and conversions from one type to another), each trying to optimise his or her MTP, in a human behavioural context. This is the basis of behavioural technical analysis.

We need to collect more evidence, and apply more verifying statistics, to refine the application of behavioural finance concepts to technical analysis, but this area is likely to prove very fruitful and may revolutionise finance and investment as we know them.

A step back from behavioural finance

So far, I have provided a concise introduction to behavioural finance, focusing on aspects which come to the fore when we are dealing with investment decisions.

Behavioural finance was classified into six categories. We first saw how human beings deal with the complexity around them. We then saw how perception and their own self play a major role in their decisions. We then looked at natural aversions, especially at investors' attitude towards risk. Finally, we looked at the influence of society and gender on decision making.

We now have to take a step back from behavioural finance in order to take a look at markets and the investment process in general. This will enable us to put behavioural finance in perspective and see how best to use it to make money by combining it with technical analysis.

There are many approaches to investment and numerous frameworks have been proposed. I am here going to write about my approach. I developed this approach over quite a number of years, studying the theory and putting it into practice. I have studied the markets, observed investors and studied many approaches to profitable investment. You may wish to use an alternative approach and this is not likely to interfere with getting the most out of the behavioural finance principles discussed in this book.

The objectives of investment

What are we trying to achieve when we invest?

We are trying to get the highest return possible in the shortest time while putting at risk the least amount of money possible.

This greedy-sounding sentence, in fact, captures the three parameters of any investment decision. These three parameters, which we will be examining in the next section, have to be evaluated and optimised whether you are buying or selling a stock, a bond, a house, a car, a factory, or, indeed, entering into any sort of venture, including embarking on a career. These three parameters are the essence of any investment decision.

The three components of any investment decision

My approach to any investment decision considers the following three aspects:

- There is always *money* or some other resource involved in investment. Money has to be committed (e.g. spent) now and recouped in the future. Investment consists of exchanging one opportunity for another. Resources always have an opportunity cost.

- *Time* is part and parcel of any decision to invest. Investment always takes place over a period of time. Investment also involves an entry at some point in time and an exit at some other point in time.

- If your trade is to be successful, *probability* should be in its favour. The investor's job is to find a high probability winning trade over a period of time.

These three aspects are often inextricably bound in any trade or investment decision.

Figure 9.1: The MTP Framework

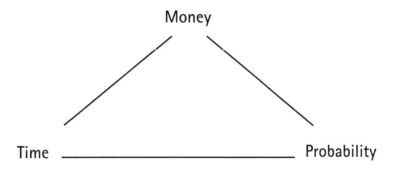

In Appendix 3 there is a list of considerations one may wish to go through to understand the structure of any investment one is contemplating.

The power of the probable

The horizon the investor has in mind determines, to a large extent, what sort of power he is looking for to move the value up (if he is taking a long position) or down (if he is taking a short position).

A day trader may be looking for fast-moving securities, or for securities making new highs or lows during the day compared to, say, the highs or lows of the day before or even earlier during the day. Alternatively, he may be looking for extremes so that he can trade against them, assuming that matters tend to reverse to normality. Or he may be attempting to 'fade the gaps', that is, looking for a rather large difference between the price the security closed at yesterday and the price it opened at today so that he can trade in the direction of yesterday's close.

A long-term investor, on the other hand, might be looking, like Warren Buffett and Charlie Munger, for companies "with a long-term competitive advantage in a stable industry" or, like Philip Fisher, for companies with the ability to keep producing growth over the foreseeable future primarily because they have good management and a good research and development programme.

Good investors are always looking for good MTP trades where money, time, and probabilities are in their favour. Whatever the M and the T components, a good investor always has to ensure that the P of the trade is right, that the trade is powered in such a way that the probability of success is in its favour.

Putting a finger on this power of the probable is the essence of investment.

The role of Mr Market

The source of the power, of course, is Mr Market.

Benjamin Graham, in *The Intelligent Investor*, speaks of Mr Market. Every day, Mr Market comes by and knocks on your door and gives you a list of prices at which he is willing to buy and sell almost any investment. You can buy from him or sell to him and, importantly, you can ignore him, day after day.

Most often, Mr Market offers you gold at the price of gold, or lead at the price of lead. Often he offers you lead at the price of gold. But, at some point, an overly depressed Mr Market comes along and knocks on your door and offers you gold for the price of lead. That day, whatever other things you have planned, ask him in, and sign a deal.

Often, though, there is some sort of hidden complication. Mr Market might be offering you gold for the price of lead but you know that, if you turn around and try to sell, you are unlikely to get a good price for gold just then. You have to wait. Before buying the gold, therefore, you have to make sure that you can sell the gold for a good price within your investment time frame.

If you are leveraged to the hilt, you may go bankrupt before you can sell the gold. Unleveraged, if you can wait ten years, then you have a good chance that you will be fine. If you can wait for twenty years, you will almost certainly be okay because each generation repeats its version of the follies.

Q: How does Mr Market arrive at a price? A: By Using SEP.

Sentiment, economics and price action: SEP

The value of any asset today is the present value of the future expected cash flow but, over time, the anticipated cash flow fluctuates as does the discount rate we feel we should apply to those cash flows. Depending on the timing of these factors, we can also arrive at future prices of an asset.

In fact, the cash flow we expect to get from any asset and the discount rate we apply depends on three factors: sentiment, economics and price action in the market. It is best to refer to these three factors by their initials, SEP. Any combination of these factors, I call an SEP set.

- We have already discussed *sentiment* at length in Chapter Seven when discussing society and the emotions which often hold sway. Sentiment here refers to both the investor's own sentiment and that of the general market.

- *Economics* includes both the fundamentals of the company concerned as well as economic prospects in general. While many industries are today global in scope, dominated by a few international companies, local factors still play an important role.

- *Price action* refers to how the price of that asset is behaving – for example, substantial price movements have a tendency to engender uptrends or downtrends while sluggish price movements make investors expect a horizontal trend.

In discussing the formation of a market avalanche in Chapter Seven, we noted that the source of the information which sets it off can be either endogenous or exogenous, coming either from inside the financial market or from outside it. The market feeds on its own price action.

Price action, of course, is not always based on economics or sentiment. Sometimes it is due to the action by a large investor or the concerted action by a group of investors in an attempt to manipulate the market and create a price movement from which they would be able to profit, in spite of strict regulations against the creation of so-called false markets.

SEP attributes a price to an asset; a spot price for a transaction now and a series of future prices. Individual opinions come to market to form market prices. SEP considerations are also responsible for changes in the price of that asset.

Importantly, changes in price, in turn, are the catalysts giving rise to the formation of new trends, the continuation of trends, and the exhaustion of trends.

Recalling that the purpose for our studying price formation is to be able to generate high probability trades, we realise that the trends resulting from changes in investors' SEP sets provide excellent opportunities because they provide an indication of direction and tend to persist for some time.

Figure 9.2: SEP and trend formation

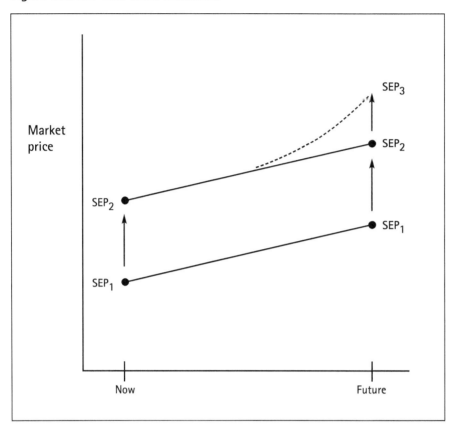

In the diagram, the asset was initially priced at SEP1, with the future price slightly higher than the spot price. Due to a change in market opinion resulting from a change in sentiment, economic circumstances or price action, SEP2 leads to a new higher price, both now and in the future. In a further twist, if market participants feel that a strong trend emerged, they might re-evaluate SEP2 and eventually adapt SEP3, thus an even higher price, by the time the future date actually arrives.

Indeed, every moment in time going forward, there are re-evaluations of SEP, changes in price, the beginning of new trends and the exhaustion of old ones.

Behavioural finance aspects of SEP

Price formation is not an objective process and is subject to most of the biases studied by behavioural finance. Similarly, our assessment of the probability of achieving a future price is susceptible to biases. This is precisely where behavioural finance departs from classical finance and the latter's dependence on rational economic man.

Obviously, sentiment is not objective. As we have seen, sentiment colours our observations and thoughts with emotion. We can be *optimistic* or *pessimistic*.[34] We can be looking at the market after sustaining heavy losses and our *loss aversion* and *regret aversion* at that point would be heightened. Alternatively, we can be looking at the market after bagging a handsome profit, at which point we are likely to be *overconfident* and high on the *illusion of control*.

These biases affect both our calculation of the likely future price at which we can hope to exit a trade and our calculation of the probabilities. After heavy losses, our price expectation and estimation of probabilities is likely to be much lower than it would be during a boom. The interpretation of economic facts, even a company's fundamentals, is often difficult. There is often a lot of data and ambiguity. Our price formation is therefore subject to *ambiguity aversion* as we try to play it safe.

Further, the biases of *recency*, *availability* and *representativeness* play a major role in how we interpret prices. Recent prices are likely to be more widely available and given greater weight in our thinking. Sometimes, movement in a popular index, such as the FTSE 100 or the S&P500, makes us assume that all the shares in the respective markets are moving when, in fact, high capitalisation stocks might be rising and the rest going nowhere. Ironically, in such a case, if we are holding a small capitalisation stock which is flat, seeing the FTSE 100 rising might serve as confirmation that we are right. The *self attribution* bias is also likely to play a role!

How we interpret economic factors and price action depends on how we *frame* them and how we *mentally account* for them. As I write, for example, I notice that market commentators are often *anchoring* prices to the March 2009 turning point – most markets started to climb back from steep falls at that point. Commentators also use past bear markets and recoveries as *stereotypes* to help them evaluate present developments.

All sorts of biases, therefore, come to bear on the how markets price assets and how investors decide on the attractiveness or otherwise of potential trades. SEP sets change continually, as do prices. As old trends terminate they are replaced by new trends, which are sustained, before they eventually come to an end as well.

To summarise this chapter so far: the objective of any investment decision is to find the best high probability trade for the time frame one has in mind and to finance the trade at the least cost. To assess the viability of trades, one has to value assets. Assets are valued on sentiment, economics and price action in the market (SEP). SEP sets change continually, thus changing expected prices. These changes in expected prices confirm old trends or create new ones, and trends provide the potential for high probability trades.

---

[34] Behavioural finance concepts have been highlighted with italics in these passages.

An approach to market structure

To invest successfully by engaging in high probability trades we have to try and understand what is happening in the market. By having a model of market structure, we can study the market's dynamics.

The three types of investor

In order to understand the role which some of the forces studied by behavioural finance have in markets, we must at this stage try to understand the behaviour of different investors and the structure of the market. What follows is not an entirely conventional explanation but it is a model which I have developed over the years and which I find useful in understanding what is happening in a specific market at a particular time.

When looking at a market, I try to deduce the behaviour and thoughts of three different types of investors.

Trend followers

First there are the trend followers. There is always a trend in the market; the market may be going up, or down, or trading horizontally.[35] Trend followers believe that the market will continue doing what it is doing.

Trend followers may be in the market or waiting to get into the market. Whether an investor is a trend follower or not is not a matter of whether the investor is participating or not at that particular time, but a matter of whether he or she believes that the present movement will continue. Someone who believes that the current trend will continue is still a trend follower even though he might not have taken a position in the market by going long or short.

Most trend followers would be participating, of course, because we are assuming that these people are investors and investors only make profits by backing their opinion with money. Non-participating investors have only incidental effects on markets.

Contrarians

The second type of investors are the contrarians. Contrarians believe that the market will change direction. They do not think that the current trend has any life left. Again, contrarians may be participating or sitting on the sidelines. If they invest, contrarian investors take a position against the market's recent direction.

---

[35] One can still make a profit if one plays a horizontal trend by trading the oscillations.

The undecided

Finally, there are the undecided. The undecided have no idea what is going to happen – the current trend might continue, or it might not. They can be in for the ride and invested in the market, either long or short, but they do not hold an opinion. Most undecideds will be out of the market.

We can construct a market matrix like this, with nine combinations:

Market matrix

	Trend follower	Contrarian	Undecided
Long	1	4	7
Short	2	5	8
Non-participating	3	6	9

Conversion

At any time, there is *conversion* between the three types of investors and there are *transactions*.

As time goes by, some trend followers become contrarians, some contrarians become trend followers, both can become undecided, and the undecided can become either trend followers or contrarians. Some participants leave the market while some non-participants enter it. In other words, conversions from one type to another are occurring all the time, as SEP sets change. There is a continual flow.

For example, the market is trending up and I think that the market is likely to continue up so I bought an exchange traded fund (ETF) for that market. I am therefore a participating trend follower with a long position. I continue to watch the market and I see some bad news and get cold feet and have doubts about the upward trend. I sell the ETF and I become a non-participating undecided since I do not have any opinion one way or the other. I sleep over it and study the market some more. I cannot come to a conclusion but the market opened strong and I do not want to miss out, so I buy into the market via the ETF again. I am a participating undecided investor with a long position. Three days later I get it in my head that the market will fall any time now. I sell my ETF at a profit. I then short the same ETF, thus becoming a participating contrarian with a short position. And so it goes on.

Let us take a closer look at the market matrix. If the trend is up, then a participating trend follower is in cell 1. If the trend is down, then the trend follower will be in cell 2. If the market is flat, a trader would either be playing the oscillations, flitting between cell 1 and cell 2, or else, if the trader thinks no profit is to be had from the oscillations, the trader might stay on the sidelines in cell 3.

Let us consider what happens when an uptrend is formed. First, let us assume that the previous trend was down. At some point, innovators in the market start believing that the current SEP set is indicating a much higher price than already exists in the market. They leave their current cell, wherever it is, and go long the market. Since the trend is still down, at this stage they are contrarians, in cell 4. As the market is re-evaluated, more investors believe that prices will go higher and join the innovators in cell 4. Eventually, the trend turns and starts going up. These innovators are now in the trend and are no longer contrarians but have become trend followers. They are now in cell 1.

More investors migrate from other cells to cell 1 and the trend will meet with confirmation and gather strength. As long as there are investors in the other cells, and as long as conversion towards cell 1 continues, the trend will continue and gather strength.

Migration from cell to cell is often accompanied by hesitancy and second thoughts. In an uptrend, for example, investors do not march from cells 2 to 9 towards cell 1 in a disciplined and ordered manner. Indeed, in most bull markets there are many reversals and many trend followers become uneasy.

As a trend develops, it is marked by patterns known as support and resistance, which we shall examine in detail later in this chapter because they provide opportunities for high probability trades. These patterns are formed as the price tries to penetrate into new ground and is thrown back. Usually, uptrends take a longer time to work through and prices are lifted gradually, while in downtrends prices drop sharply and rapidly.

Figure 9.3: Types of Investors

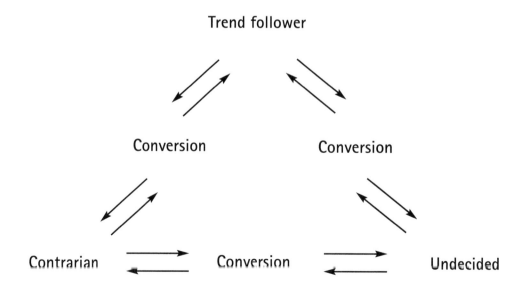

The composition of the market changes all the time. In most markets there is a balance between the three types of investors, some of whom are participating while others are waiting to participate. Observers who never participate are not investors but may influence a market in other ways, e.g. by commenting publicly.

This discussion on trend followers, contrarians and the undecided ties in with George Soros' insight that, at any one time, either the market, we as investors, or both, can be right or wrong. When we are in agreement with the market, we are trend followers; when not, contrarians. Sometimes we just don't know.

News, conversion and volatility

Various studies have shown that trading volume is positively correlated with the volatility of a security's price; that is, when trading volume increases, so does the variability of price. This does not mean that volume causes volatility but that there are likely to be common factors which affect both volume and volatility.

In the market matrix context, news and uncertainty causes investors to re-assess the price derived from their perception of the SEP set and this, in turn, causes conversion to speed up – investors start moving between the cells much faster when there is news or heightened uncertainty. Volatility therefore increases as the price varies. At the same time, the conversions taking place push up volume.

In this way, the market matrix suggests an explanation of why trading volume and volatility are positively correlated.

A note on the undecided

One must not deride the undecided. Indeed, many pure trend followers insist that they do not even wish to have an opinion on the market's direction. Some don't even read financial news. They insist that the economy and markets are too complex for anyone to fathom and all they hope to do is ride trends. So they just focus on what the market is doing and concentrate on going long, short or staying out of the market.

One thing about the undecided that is certainly positive is that they do not put their ego on the line. They do not fear being proven wrong nor are they in danger of succumbing to hubris when they are right. Rather, they retain full flexibility, a freedom which often distinguishes winners from losers.

We will now examine three technical analysis tools – extremes, trends, and support and resistance – and their behavioural finance roots.

Extremes

Whether one is looking at a market or a security over a number of years, months, days, or even hours, it becomes clear that prices periodically go to extremes, either on the high side or the low side. Extreme prices are marked by spikes because the price reverses sharply.

Again, the biases of *recency* and *availability* play a strong role in the formation of extremes. The rush to be long or short the market and follow the obtaining trend would not only be recent but probably even reported in the news, thus widely available.

The success of those joining the trend encourages *herding* and with success comes a lot of *self attribution* and *illusion of control* which reinforces the trend. Previous losses are ignored and one tends to *frame* the rush of prices to the extreme on its own. Traders *overreact* to the trend and accord it a greater probability of continuation even though it is approaching extreme levels. To traders, the trend is a *heuristic* by which they understand what is happening and a heuristic is never abandoned easily.

The sharp reversal is caused by the *disposition effect*: as the movement extends itself, investors start to get anxious about losing their profits and some start selling. The price movement itself, the third component of SEP, provides a cue to other investors and they too sell their holdings. The price drops rapidly, often going to the opposite extreme. *Recency* and *availability* then start working in the opposite direction. This to-and-fro movement is a feature of any market; the freer a market is, the quicker it reacts back and forth.

An extreme may signal a change in trend. In such cases, the price reverses and never comes back to continue the original trend. Trend turning points are often formed by a series of extreme points forming rather wide oscillations.

A reversal from an extreme point, however, does not always signify a change in the overall trend. It often just indicates that the price has run ahead of the trend and is snapped back within the fold.

Extremes are fascinating to study and can form the basis of some very high probability trades but they are very fleeting and require quite a lot of training to identify correctly and capture in time.

Trends

Technical analysis can be said to be the study of trends. Technical analysis books deal with such topics as:

- What is a trend?

- What is the direction of the trend?

- Is it a strong or a weak trend?

- When is the trend likely to turn?

- What happens when the trend turns?

The trend, I think, has the soundest basis of all technical analysis techniques and has been successfully applied by a multitude of investors.[36]

The trend is the direction of the market, which way the price is moving. Specifically, an uptrend is a series of higher peaks and higher troughs while a downtrend is a series of lower peaks and lower troughs.

What the trend is depends on the time frame one is using. Looking at prices over a week could indicate an uptrend but looking at the same prices in the context of a month could show a downtrend. Over a whole year, again, the trend could be up. The time frame that a particular set of investors adopt depends on their MTP framework – the period over which they seek to make money. Other periods may also be studied for the information they contain. In fact, looking at prices over multiple time frames is widely used in technical analysis.

Trends tend to persist and create their own strength. As Larry Williams stated:

> The most compelling thing I find in the marketplace technically is trend. I know price causes trend, but I also think trend causes price and that if a market is in a big down trend prices just keep going down.

The trend follower/contrarian/undecided model of market structure focuses on the current trend. Investors are either participating or not, and they are either followers, contrarians or undecided.

It is therefore important that we examine in some detail the behavioural finance aspects of trends, on which the model rests.

---

[36] For investors interested in trend following trading methods, a good place to start is Michael Covel's *Trend Following*. Covel is currently one of the main proponent of trend investing. He has recently chronicled the history of the Turtles, one of the successful trend-following trading teams.

Behavioural finance and trends

As we saw in Chapter Three, human beings attempt to simplify the great complexity around them. We saw that one way they do this is by using *heuristics*, or rules of thumb, in order to immediately resolve an issue.

One of the most powerful heuristics is the trend. People observe what is happening and decide that what is happening now will continue to happen. A trend once started, therefore, has a tendency to continue. Like members of any society, investors tend to herd and follow the direction set by the crowd. Thus Lord Keynes said: "Worldly wisdom teaches that it is better for reputation to fail conventionally than to succeed unconventionally."

The trend heuristic is buttressed by the *recency bias*; our tendency to think that what has happened recently is bound to keep repeating. What happened recently is remembered clearly and is likely to be the first thing which comes to mind when we come to decide where to invest.

Further, what is happening now, or what has just happened, is likely to have more coverage in the media around us than what happened in the past, and that means that our brains are more exposed to what is happening now than what happened in the past. Our *availability bias*, therefore, takes hold and we assume that what we see best represents reality.

Trend followers tend to suffer from *selective perception* and be susceptible to the *confirmation bias* once a trend takes shape. Information which supports our beliefs is given importance while conflicting information is ignored.

Trend followers, therefore, will tend to *underreact* to what does not fall within the pattern. At the same time, observations which fall in line come to represent reality, an aspect of our *representativeness bias*. Observations which fit in this way also feed our *illusion of control*.

Investors' vision is somewhat compromised too because we have a tendency to make decisions depending on the context in which the alternatives are framed, our *framing bias*. Since we are looking at recent history and what is happening now, the trend dominates our frame.

Once a trend is formed it tends to snowball by converting contrarians and the undecided into trend followers. These conversions give strength to the trend and trend followers' *confirmation* and *recency biases* push them towards *overconfidence*.

Trend followers would be reluctant to abandon a heuristic which worked so well. When, eventually, the trend starts to weaken, many trend followers *underreact* to the news, thus dissipating contrarians' strength.

A trend tends to persist longer than the fundamentals indicate because, as we have seen, economics is just one component of the price setting mechanism. The other two components in SEP are sentiment and price action, and both of these would be in favour of the trend for quite some time after it starts to weaken. This overshooting is a good place to stack probabilities in your favour.

Here I have discussed the behavioural finance aspects of an uptrend, and mostly from the point of view of trend followers. Many of the biases discussed, of course, would also be affecting contrarians or the undecided. Each looks at the evidence from his or her own perspective.

If a trend is joined by all investors, that is, if all investors participate as trend followers, then the trend changes because there are no new entrants. For example, if there is an uptrend, and all investors buy the stock, the stock cannot keep moving up. It will flatten and eventually fall as some holders are forced by circumstances to sell, e.g. to buy a house or pay college fees.

A case study

The following graph shows the S&P 500, a stock index published by Standard & Poor's consisting of the 500 largest capitalisation stocks traded on the New York Stock Exchange and NASDAQ in the United States.

Figure 9.4: S&P 500 September 1995 to October 2009

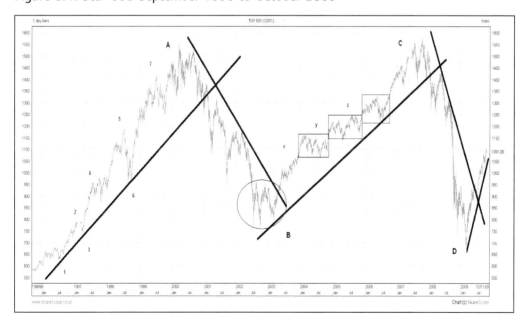

I chose this period because it provides us with a very good example of how trends form, continue, go to extremes, and reverse to form new trends.

First, notice the five straight lines showing the main trends over the last fourteen years. The last trend, starting on 10 March 2009, is still relatively short, of course.

There are four turning points, marked A to D. The last turning point, D, is very sharp and is marked by the extreme reading of 676 on 9 March. A, B, and C, on the other hand, consist of two or three extreme readings and wild oscillations. One can best see the oscillations at B.

On the left hand side, I have marked some of the extremes which did not result in a change in trend. These are marked 1 to 7. Note that these extremes are as sharp (and as profitable!) as the extremes in A to D but reversals against the trend from points 2, 4, 5, and 7 faltered while reversals in favour of the trend from points 1, 3, and 6 continued.

If we look at the trend between 2003 (point B) and 2007 (point C) we notice the areas marked X, Y, and Z. These are support and resistance areas.[37] Notice how the top of X forms the bottom of Y and how the top of Y forms the bottom of Z. Within each of the boxes, we can see the price oscillating until it finally breaks through to the next level. We can see similar support and resistance boxes on all the trends because this is how trends move.

Support and resistance provides various opportunities for high probability trades. They also provide good guidance as to when to join a trend.

I will examine the behavioural finance aspects of support and resistance later in this chapter.

Figure 9.5: S&P 500 January 2009 to October 2009

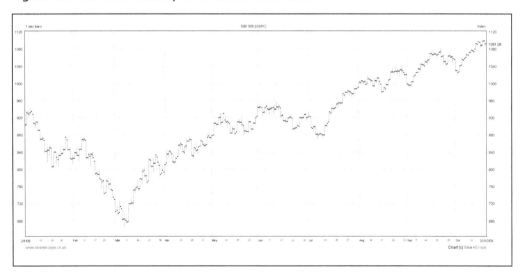

---

[37] Support and resistance are often referred to as lines but I prefer to think of them as areas because the precise point of reversal varies.

Figure 9.6: S&P 500 March 2009 to October 2009

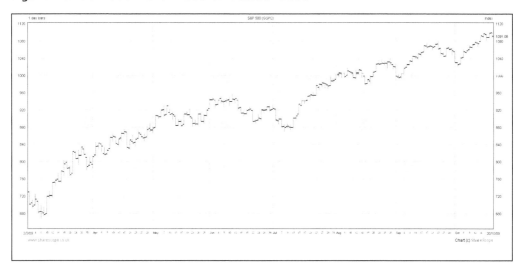

Finally, look at the two diagrams of the S&P 500 in Figure 9.5 and Figure 9.6. The first is for January 2009 to October 2009 while the second shows only the index between March 2009 and October 2009.

Figure 9.5 shows a fall from around 930 in January to 676 in March and then a climb to around 1070. But hearing commentators in October 2009, many are looking at the rise since the lows of March. This is the subject of the second graph. Notice how steep the rise now looks. I call this frame imposition because commentators and other analysts would be imposing their own time frame on the market and reaching conclusions based on this time frame. Imposed time frames usually hang on market turning points.

Avoiding frame imposition lies behind one of the tenets of technical analysis, namely, that price movements should always be analysed at different time frames.

Support and resistance

> "I generally prefer to set my stops based on technical support and resistance levels in the chart of the underlying security."
>
> Lawrence G. McMillan, *McMillan on Options*

Support and resistance, usually taken together as one price pattern, is one of the key concepts in technical analysis because it has strong descriptive powers and, in the hands of an able technician, considerable predictive ones.

The pattern explains how a stock is moving now and within which limits it is likely to move in the near future. Support and resistance works well at different timescales, whether one is day trading or investing for the medium or long term.

Support and resistance illustrates how cognitive and emotional heuristics play a major role in price pattern formation and this is the central postulate of behavioural technical analysis.

Notice, as you go through the following graphs, that support and resistance areas themselves are made up of prices going to extremes and snapping back. This is true whatever the timescale one is using – whether over a week, a day, an hour, or a few minutes. What distinguishes a support and resistance area is that this to-and-fro motion of extremes takes place within a rather small, confined area.

To illustrate, I have chosen a practical example of the pattern emerging in a real market. Figure 9.7 is a price graph of Lloyds Banking Group plc shares between the start of 2003 and the end of 2007.[38]

---

[38] Previously Lloyds TSB Group.

Figure 9.7: Lloyds Banking Group 2003-2007

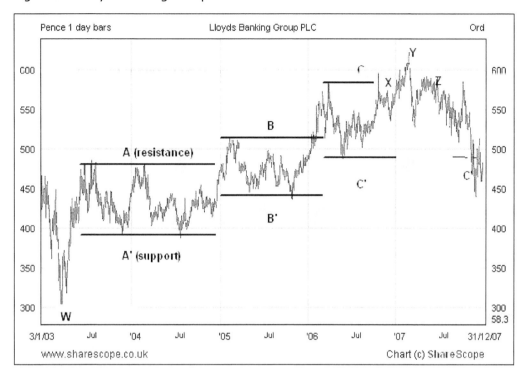

The price action prior to the period shown in the diagram was as follows. From its relative closing high of GBP 8.17 reached in May 2002, the stock fell precipitously to just under GBP 3 in mid-March 2003, the point marked W in Figure 9.7. Point W was quite an overreaction for Lloyds shares since these levels were last seen in 1996, seven years before!

We have seen, earlier in this book, how markets tend to underreact at first and then, in a period of wild adjustments, to overreact. This was a clear instance of where one could pick up a great bargain.

Contrarians, as bargain hunters, very quickly did the honours and turned the trend sharply at W, pushing up the share to the first support and resistance area in the graph, the one sandwiched between line A and A', with a price between GBP 4 and GBP 4.80.

In this trading range, one could see the struggle between old contrarians, now trend followers, wanting to push the price further up, and the new contrarians who thought that at anywhere over GBP 4.50 the price had come up too quickly.

The glass ceiling

The line marked A shows the resistance line while the line marked A' shows the support line. Resistance implies that there is a glass ceiling at around that level preventing the price from reaching any higher. Support implies a floor which prevents the price from falling further.[39]

Usually, support and resistance lines are parallel but we have to have some artistic licence in marking where they lie because, of course, prices tend to cluster around a notional line rather than totally respect it. The distance between the lines can also vary quite widely.

We can see that between May 2003 and the end of 2004, for twenty months, the share price stayed within the support and resistance area denoted by AA'. In the meantime, the market, as measured in this case by the FTSE 100, climbed slowly.

Many things are taking place when a market is trading sideways, as in this case, even though it appears that the share price is going nowhere.

Applying behavioural finance to support and resistance

During the first part of the enveloped phase, contrarians who had missed buying at point W would be waiting for the price to fall back again. They would be suffering from *regret* that they had not bought when the price was so low. For now, these new trend followers would stay on the sidelines. One dominating bias would be *loss aversion* – they want to see the price fall before they commit their money, fearing that it might fall again to the GBP 3 level, or even further. Remember that the share price had fallen by more than 60%, from GBP 8.17 to GBP 3. Who's to say it won't fall again?

As soon as the price started to recover from GBP 3, *get-evenitis* came into play. People holding shares as the price plummeted might have resolved to get rid of the shares as soon as the price recovered. They had suffered a lot of pain and their *regret* must have been sky high. They got their cue when the share price hit GBP 4.80. At that point they started selling, thus forming the resistance line A.

With these sales, the price fell back. People who had missed the chance to buy at GBP 3 and saw the share go up to GBP 4.80 were regretting their decision even more and resolved to buy shares when they fell somewhat and now, with the price just above GBP 4, they saw their chance, and bought, thus forming line A'.

They may have reasoned – as is quite common – that it would be unlikely for the price to fall below GBP 4. Why GBP 4? It is the next round number from GBP 3. This may sound frivolous but, in fact, support and resistance levels tend to form at round numbers.

---

[39] Keep in mind, however, that a very strong market can push the price through support and resistance levels rather easily. In market studies, there are very few, if any, absolutes.

The reader would suspect, rightly, that there are a lot of conversions between the three types of investors as the market behaves in this way, forming support and resistance levels.

Entrenchment

We can see how the share price fluctuated between the limits indicated by lines A and A' and how this range held for some twenty months. During those twenty months, of course, the share price was pretty much anchored there. That range became a sort of *status quo* for the share price and conservative investors would not have taken easily to an idea of a much higher or a much lower price, at least in the short and medium term. The new range became the recent range, benefitting from the *recency bias*, and it mitigated the previous behaviour, that of the precipitous fall.

During these twenty months, the share price stabilised. The investors involved in Lloyds – long, short, or just watching – had the time to pin down a price, get over their regret, and get over their attacks of *get-evenitis*. Traders don't much like sideways movements, because they cannot usually make much money, unless they trade the oscillations, buying at A' and selling at A, but actually sideways movement can be good to have. Certain trading strategies, for example, make it a condition that a trader gets involved in a security only after it has gone through a period of consolidation.

Changing roles

To continue, the ceiling at GBP 4.80 was broken early in 2005 when the resistance line went up to around the GBP 5 level. This turned out to be an extremely important level, as we shall see.

One notices that while the resistance line stepped up only a little, from A to B, the support line went up quite a distance, from A' to B'. We now have a new support and resistance area BB'.

As soon as the resistance line at A was broken, and the share price went up to about GBP 5.10, there was substantial selling which might have been caused by the *disposition effect* taking hold of those investors who might have been sitting on capital gains and were waiting to collect the dividend declared at the time, one amounting to 23 pence per share, before booking in a tidy profit in quite a short period of time.

Notice that the new support line, at B', is quite close to the level of the old resistance line at A. This is quite a usual occurrence. When a share price is increasing, the old resistance line usually becomes the new support line. When a share is falling, the old support line becomes the new resistance line. This is shown in Figure 9.8.

Figure 9.8: support and resistance line changing roles

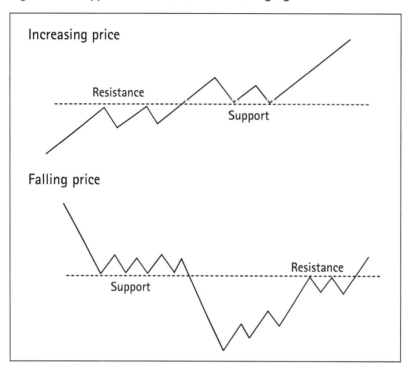

The changing roles of the support and resistance lines may be due to the *conservatism* and *recency biases* making investors cling on to the old anchored resistance line when there is a rising trend and to the old anchored support line in a downtrend. Anchors, once formed, are hard to abolish and tend to persist by changing roles from resistance lines to support lines when the price is rising, and from support lines to resistance lines when the price is falling.

Prior to the development of behavioural finance concepts, support and resistance was normally explained by noting that as the price of an asset (stocks, commodities, houses) breaks out of its prior price range, there is traders' remorse: buyers think they paid too much, sellers that they got too little. Both wish to reverse their prior decision. The price falls to its previous range when both buyers and sellers come to their senses.

Looking at the Lloyds share price in Figure 9.7, we see that consolidation did not take as long as the first one, one year in the case of BB' compared to twenty months in case of AA'. The anchors, at lines B and B', were rather close to the previous lines and therefore the mental adjustments required, by the generally conservative market participants, were not too large.

Again, starting early in 2006, the price formed another support and resistance area, between the resistance line at C and the support line at C'. Notice that the disposition effect was still in effect, with the price forming two peaks on the C line and then falling back, with people taking profit.

Also notice how, this time, the new support line at C' is very close to the old resistance line B. This is the round number GBP 5.

The share had performed very well, up from GBP 3 in 2003 to GBP 5.50 in 2006, an increase of 37% in price plus a handsome dividend averaging around 6% per annum.

This run started being reversed in late 2006 and early 2007 when the head-and-shoulder formation marked by points X, Y, and Z was formed. After that, as we know, all banks' share prices plummeted. The price sliced down through all previous support levels.

The price graph of Lloyds, like many others, shows a story of profit-pleasure-seeking and loss-pain-avoidance, underpinned by the various heuristics and effects, both emotional and cognitive, which are the subject matter of behavioural finance. The principles discussed are of universal application.

Surprise and revision

Now the carrot and the stick come into the picture. If you get it right, you make a profit, and a profit is pleasurable. This is the carrot. If you get it wrong, you make a loss, and a loss is painful. The stick.

So the market has an inbuilt auto-correcting mechanism. If you turn out to be wrong, you underreact at first, but you underreact less the second time you're wrong, and even less the third time, and so on, until you change your expectations and come in line with the market.

If you started out on the right side of the market, or if you are agile enough in revising your initially wrong position, you will capture the risk premium for yourself and make a profit. So, as an investor, you are always trying to be in line with what is going to actually happen; in other words, you are trying to guess right.

Whatever happens, as soon as your new stance delivers profit, you would tend to become conservative with regards to your new stance. When the market changes once again, there is once more the tendency to *underrate* the news at first, and *under react*, and suffer a loss. The pain of this loss makes you revise your expectations until you are back in line; you make a profit but then conservatism takes over again, the market changes, you are not quick enough to change, and you make a loss. And so it goes on.

Actually, in real life, things get even more interesting than this because sometimes, rather than underrate and underreact we do the opposite – that is, we *overrate* and *overreact*!

We must first note that both underreaction and overreaction stem from *overconfidence.* Whether we go over or whether we go under, we do so because we think we are right, we believe we know.

It is our reaction to surprise which determines whether we then underrate and underreact or whether we are so startled that we overrate that piece of news and overreact. It depends on the circumstances, the extent of the movement which led to the surprise, what is happening around us, and our adrenaline and nerves.

It is always hard to tell what the reaction will be and the market often reacts to the same kind of news in a different manner. There is a tendency, however, for a certain kind of news to attract more attention than another.

Many investors, for example, underreact to analysts' recommendations. Investors also often underreact to revisions of financial figures resulting from changes in accounting regulations as well as to write-offs against profit of items which investors already knew about, such as goodwill. On the other hand, in my experience, investors overreact to Initial Public Offerings (IPO).

The investment process

Figure 9.9 shows what might be taking place in markets by looking at the investment process from the point of view of a typical investor who, in this example, has arrived at an opinion that the current uptrend will continue This diagram is highly stylised and lacks the dynamism we find in the real world, but it may help illustrate the process:

Figure 9.9: The investment process of a participating trend follower

Investor wants to make a profit or avoid a loss

Investor forms an opinion on the market,

for example by analysing the market (fundamental analysis),

seeking opinions (availability bias),

looking at price trends and indicators (technical analysis),

looking at recent market performance (recency bias),

looking for cues in certain companies (representativeness bias).

By thus considering sentiment, economics and price action (SEP),

the investor arrives at an opinion of an asset's price.

This price is above the current price so the investor expects the current uptrend to continue.

↓

Investor anchors his opinion

↓

Investor feels a vested interest in the work he has carried out.

He thinks he has figured the market out (illusion of control)

and seeks to preserve the status quo

and is conservative.

↓

Investor feels confident enough that the current trend will continue (trend follower) and takes a position in the market seeking to capture a profit by utilising his newly acquired knowledge.

Endowment bias sets in.

↓

Investor makes a profit or a loss.

Success makes him over-confident.

Failure can make him lose confidence and maybe overrate the news.

Or he may stick to his original opinion until its time comes around,

and so underrates the news.

Investor continues to want to make a profit or avoid a loss.

Mental accounting may be deceptive.

Investor adjusts the anchor.

Investor makes a profit or a loss.

Investor may meet with success or failure again.

Underrating or overrating leading to a dynamic

process of underreaction and overreaction.

Investor continues to want to make a profit or avoid a loss.

Investor adjusts the anchor.

The process iterates

The market fluctuates.

The investor overreacts and underreacts,

making profits and losses.

Behavioural models

Price trend analysis combined with support and resistance is used by floor traders, day traders, commodity traders and stock traders, in the short, medium and long term. These techniques can be the basis of profitable trading since they tilt the probabilities towards their skilful user. I here discuss the behavioural finance dynamics of these two patterns.

At the existing state of knowledge, the interpretation of what is taking place in the mind of the individual investor, or of groups of investors, cannot but contain a large amount of subjectivity, but by keeping behavioural finance concepts in mind we can interpret what is going on in the market accurately.

As we shall see in Chapter Ten, behavioural finance concepts are continually being researched and new findings, provisionally validating or rejecting hypotheses, have to be integrated into technical analysis to enhance our understanding. Eventually, as new findings allow us to better integrate behavioural finance with technical analysis, the predictive value of behavioural technical analysis will increase. At this stage, this integration has just started.

Since our aim is to have the probabilities work in our favour, one of the main roles of behavioural finance should be to discover the foundations of technical analysis so that technical analysis can provide its students with more trades that have a high probability of winning. This is the combined approach I have been referring to as behavioural technical analysis.

Researchers often use behavioural finance concepts to explain price patterns being investigated. For example, various studies have shown that stock prices exhibit intermediate-term (3 to 12 months) momentum and long-term reversals; in the intermediate-term, prices continue rolling on their previous path but then, after a year, they reverse direction and go in the opposite direction to the previous trend. These studies – see Jegadeesh and Titman, as an example – show what happens if we buy winners and sell losers. Others – George and Hwang – focus on the nearness of the price to the 52-week high. Park studied the position of the 50-day moving average versus the 200-day moving average.

Various behavioural finance concepts are referred to in order to explain why stocks selected by these three methods exhibit similar patterns of intermediate-term momentum and long-term reversal. Reference is made to overconfidence, conservatism, anchoring, overreaction and underreaction. Park, in his paper, gives a good summary of the research findings and the possible behavioural finance dynamics at play.

This area is one of the better integrated fields and shows the great practical potential of combining technical analysis with behavioural finance.

Analysing the market

In analysing a market, it is helpful to keep the three types of investors in mind. Ask yourself:

- What is the trend right now?
- What are trend followers/contrarians thinking?
- What are trend followers/contrarians expecting to happen?
- Are these expectations borne out by the fundamentals?
- Are these expectations widespread?
- What's the best/worst thing that can happen to trend followers/contrarians?
- Is new money entering the market?
- Is the trend in volume the same or counter to the trend in prices?
- For example, if we saw a week of uptrend in the stock market, did today's volume increase prices or reduce them?[40]
- What are most non-participating investors thinking and feeling? Are they on the sidelines with lots of cash or is participation at a high level?
- Do similar markets give any hints as to what is happening to the three types of investors in this market?

These and similar questions will help you understand what is happening and collect the pertinent statistics. Each question suggests others and together they help you get at a reasonable idea of what may be happening in the market.

It is therefore important to always try to have an idea of the extent of participation in a market – whether there is a lot of participation or whether many investors are sitting on the sidelines. This is often not easy to do and can rarely be done accurately.

Researchers often conduct surveys among investors to see who is a bull, a bear or undecided. As far as I know, none of them survey the nine cells of the market matrix presented earlier, but one can gain some understanding of the structure of the market at any one time by studying other statistics.

Stock exchanges publish data of new highs and new lows, the number of shares increasing in price and those falling, the percentage of shares above certain moving averages, volumes of trades, etc. Similarly, many futures and options exchanges and regulatory agencies publish a lot of detailed and timely data, including changes in open interest, how many long and short futures contracts are held by different types of participant and the number of calls versus puts. All these statistics help.

---

[40] You can measure this by calculating the volume of transactions of increasing shares versus total volume.

I also use the MTP framework to analyse a proposed investment and impose discipline. By listing the main components of the MTP framework for each deal, such as that presented in the checklist in Appendix 3, one would know from where one started and know what one is proposing to change as time goes by.[41]

The MTP framework connects to the three types of investors because these three make up the market and the market not only determines the probabilities but often the time frame as well. There is also a link to the money aspect of MTP because resources are traded differently and markets have different statistical characteristics.[42]

Primary observations of this chapter

To help you in your trading, these are this chapter's main observations:

1. Any market can be seen as consisting of trend followers, contrarians and undecided investors who may be participating or non-participating. These form the market matrix. Investors seek profit via money-time-probability (MTP) decisions.

2. Asset prices are determined by sentiment, economics and price action (SEP).

3. If a trend emerges, the greater the proportion of investors who are undecided, or even contrarian, the better the prospects for that trend because there is a bigger pool from which conversions can take place. (Mixed comments are good news.) As a corollary: if a trend emerges, the greater the proportion of trend followers, the worse the prospects for that trend. (Agreement is bad news.)

4. Liquidity in the market encourages the conversion of non-participating investors into participating investors with a bias to the long side (uptrend). As a corollary: lack of liquidity in the market encourages the conversion of participating into non-participating investors with a bias to the short side (downtrend).

5. When a special time frame emerges, what I call *frame imposition*, the trend would be seen in that frame. A special time frame is usually anchored on a major turning point. In the absence of a special time frame, a calendar year time frame is normally used. A time frame may help or hinder a trend.

6. Trends make progress in a series of support and resistance patterns. Such patterns consist of extremes and reversals.

7. At all time frames, trends go to extremes. All extremes reverse but not all reversals lead to a new trend.

---

[41] Change and flexibility are important in investment. Our aim is to make a profit, not to have guessed right at the start.

[42] Certain systems, for example, work well on currencies or commodities but not on stocks, and vice versa.

Key concepts in this chapter

- Sentiment, economics, price action (SEP)
- Trend followers, contrarians, undecided
- Market matrix
- Money, time, and probabilities (the MTP Framework)
- Trends
- Extreme prices and reversals
- Support and resistance
- Frame imposition
- Behavioural technical analysis
- Underreaction and overreaction

Chapter Ten –
New Horizons

"We don't receive wisdom; we discover it for ourselves after a journey that no one can take for us or spare us."

Marcel Proust

What this chapter is about

This concluding chapter looks at the various approaches to understanding *economic energy* in order to make better investment decisions: fundamental, technical and quantitative analysis.

Throughout history, investors' concerns have remained very much the same. Modern researchers are working on one of the main concerns of Robert Rhea, one of the fathers of Dow Theory, who wrote 70 years ago.

Infusing behavioural finance into technical analysis and marshalling empirical and statistical evidence stands a good chance of generating big steps in investment. This should be the main goal of behavioural technical analysis.

Fundamental, technical and quantitative finance

In a way, investment can be looked at as the management of *economic energy*. In the same way that physical energy can be created and stored, and used to power movement and light, the economy can be said to create energy as entrepreneurs build wealth, people work, credit is created, and money shifts from one asset to another. Asset prices move in response to economic energy.

As its name implies, fundamental analysis looks at the basic economic building blocks to study how economic energy builds up. Analysts examine companies and the economies within which the companies operates and form a reasoned judgement of how things are likely to develop, of companies' business prospects and likely future profits, and thus the developments in the prices of these companies.

Profit associated with an asset might take years to generate a movement in that asset's price and this is where technical analysis comes in. Technical analysis studies actual movements in price to try and figure out where prices are likely to go. It looks at the patterns of price movements as well as various indicators which measure different aspects of these price movements.

Quantitative finance can be said to be the statistical analysis of market phenomena – a modelling of the manifestations. It is a very powerful approach. Quantitative finance does not study the patterns of price movement as such, but how price movements are distributed statistically; and this is then used to construct a model to help explain the market. Observed phenomena, market dicta[43] and behavioural finance biases are tested in the most scientific way that the markets and the data will allow.

---

[43] Such as 'Sell in May and come back on Michaelmas day'.

Three pillars

These three disciplines – fundamental, technical and quantitative analysis – are the three pillars on which modern finance rests.

The introduction of behavioural finance into modern finance adds insight into what moves markets by examining how market participants make decisions. The manifestation of the market can then be interpreted more meaningfully.

Fundamental economic developments still determine performance over the longer term and it is difficult to see how one can invest over the longer term without reference to how the fundamentals are shaping up.

Importantly, however, the manifestation of these fundamental economic forces in asset price movements – the stuff on which technical and quantitative analysis is built – depends on how human beings, the building blocks of the market, make their financial decisions.

The integration of behavioural finance with the manifestation of asset price movement and their objective testing according to the scientific method will generate an avalanche of research, transforming most of what we know about finance.

Figure 10.1: Behavioural technical analysis

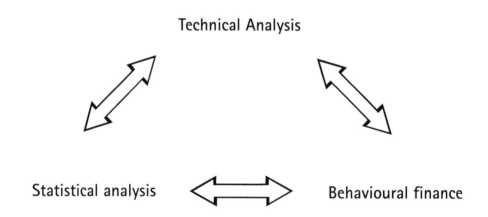

Behavioural technical analysis will involve unearthing the driving forces of technical analysis with the use of behavioural finance observations and statistical analysis in order to generate effective high probability winning trades.

The technicians

I started out as a fundamental analyst and came to technical analysis after reading behavioural finance because I realised that if participants are driving the market then we must first study investors' behaviour in the market as revealed by securities prices in technical analysis.

It is interesting to note how this approach to investing has thrown up the same challenges to its students across the years. During my research for this book, I came across the two following examples.

Compare the two extracts. In each I have italicised the important words.

First, from page 8 of Richard Russell's book *The Dow Theory Today*.[44] This extract is from a letter of Russell's written in 1958, in which he quotes Robert Rhea:

> Again, said Rhea, 'the final stage is sometimes recognisable because people then buy stocks *simply because they go up*, and *because other people are buying them*. They consider it old-fashioned to regard earnings or prospects.'

Now, fast forward 70 years from Rhea's time, or 50 years from Russell's letter, to 2007.

The second extract, from the abstract and the introduction to a paper by Kallinterakis and Leite Ferreira entitled 'Herding and Positive Feedback Trading in the Portuguese Stock Exchange: An Exploratory Investigation':

> Our research attempts to address two aspects of this convergence [of investors' beliefs and actions], *namely positive feedback trading ('trend-chasing')* and *herding*. Using data from the Portuguese PSI-20 market index herding appears to be rising during periods of 'definitive' market direction and exhibits descending tendencies during periods of market fluctuations. Results indicate the significance of herding and positive feedback trading towards the index, both of which appear to be experiencing a sharp rise between 1996 and 1999. This coincides with the Portuguese market's 'boom-bust' in the second half of the 1990s.

The following is from the introduction, to explain the terms:

> *Positive feedback trading* relates to the practice of following past price patterns (De Long, Shleifer, Summers and Waldman, 1990). *Herding*, on the other hand, pertains to collective behavioural phenomena, where people imitate the decisions of others (Devenow and Welch, 1996). A positive feedback trader, trades towards the direction suggested by historical prices, while a person who herds follows the actions of others.

---

[44] Dow Theory, which falls in and out of favour, has been described by Edwards and Magee as being "the granddaddy of all technical market studies." It is primarily a trend identification system. Russell still writes and publishes his Dow Theory Letters from which his book was compiled.

I have presented this comparison to show, first, how similar the concerns of traders across the decades are and, second, to give an example of how modern research, especially in behavioural finance, is endeavouring to elucidate and verify concepts which traders arrived at empirically. This would make for better investment decision making.

Putting a system together

When analysing the price action in any market, it is important to keep in mind the six main behavioural finance concepts covered in the first part of this book as well as the approach discussed in Chapter Nine.

For your convenience I have prepared a list of biases and heuristics showing the pages in this book where they are discussed as well as their nature, that is, whether they are primarily cognitive or emotional. This list can be found in Appendix 2. It would be helpful, when interpreting a market's movements, to go through the list and see which concepts are relevant at any one time. Why are investors reacting as they are? How are they likely to react in the near future?

Keep in mind that the price of a security is not arrived at by rational robots analysing purely economic data but by human beings who weigh the merits of economic data – which is often conflicting – with the price action they perceive and within the context of the dominant sentiment. This is captured by SEP.

SEP contains a strong emotional component via sentiment and investors' reactions to price movement. This demarcates behavioural technical analysis from classical finance and even, to some extent, from traditional technical analysis with its focus on price action. Keep SEP in mind when trying to deduce how the market is arriving at prices.

High probability trades

The money-time-probability framework shows how important it is to analyse these three components of any trade. We have to especially make sure that we are getting into a high probability trade – that is, a trade statistically favoured by the probable – rather than one based on vague forecasts or unfounded recommendations.

The level of probability we are looking for often determines what money we can use and the time frame, but all three are interdependent.

It is often assumed that high probability trades carry a low return because of the belief that only by taking high risk can one get a high return, but return is not always proportional to risk, as most of economics assumes. For example, just because you invest in stocks does not mean that you are going to do better than if you invest in bonds. Similarly, don't assume that illiquid investments have higher returns than liquid ones. You are not always paid extra for locking your money away. Put each deal through the MTP filter.

In studying a market, try to always be alert for data which indicates the market's structure as shown in the market matrix. I find the matrix to be extremely useful as a frame on which to hang statistics, comments and market action. The market matrix, as we saw in Chapter Nine, is fully supported by behavioural finance concepts.

The market matrix, in turn, explains how we get what I consider to be the three main sources of high probability trades: trends, extremes and support and resistance.

A trader can start with, say, one of the three graph patterns in Chapter Nine or any other pattern which the trader thinks tilts the odds in his favour, and go on from there.

For example, if you are interested in developing further the trend and support and resistance patterns which I discussed in the previous chapter, you can start by reading books about these two patterns and looking up finance research on the topic. A good place to start is with Brock, Lakonishok and LeBaron's paper entitled 'Simple Technical Trading Rules and the Stochastic Properties of Stock Returns' which appeared in *The Journal of Finance* in 1992, and which tests various versions of trading rules based on trending and price breakouts of support and resistance. With Brock et al's paper you would already have something to work on and refine – please always do your own testing and verification – and I hope that once you delve into the literature you would find that this book helps you understand the behaviour behind the patterns.

Alternative trading systems and strategies

Before investing time and effort, alternative trading strategies and systems need to be assessed for probabilities. It is here that experience in trading environments and trading coaches comes in very useful since they help point a new trader in the right direction. The system one eventually settles on depends a lot on one's personality.

My studies in technical analysis and behavioural finance, for example, enabled me to put together systems which make use of both trend following and contrarian methods and apply them to various instruments depending on market conditions. I continually research and test ideas which are related to the systems in order to keep refining them.

The trader can put the different elements of the chosen system within the MTP framework for better understanding. The trader can put together what's taught about the pattern he is seeking to exploit in the investment classics and textbooks, study the behavioural finance literature which impinges on the pattern, look up academic research, marshal the tools available, analyse the typical behaviour of the three types of investors in such a formation, and test his system thoroughly, both on paper and by actual trading in the market with small positions.

Learning a lot about one particular approach or pattern, gaining experience using it, assessing it frequently, and absorbing and adapting new research findings and tools into the method, usually works better than flitting from one approach to the other.

This book will have served its purpose if readers gain a better appreciation of the wide implications of behavioural finance and how it can be combined with technical analysis within the MTP framework to deliver wealth gains.

Key concepts in this chapter

- Economic energy
- Fundamental, technical and quantitative analysis
- Behavioural technical analysis

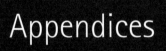

Appendices

Appendix One –
Rational Economic Man

Rational economic man

Economists, in building their models, assume a lot of things about economic agents.

Most of economics was for a long time based on the fundamental assumption that human beings are rational, know all there is to know about goods and services, and possess infinite instantaneous computing power. When acting economically, human beings try to reach goals in the most efficient way, and that involving the least cost. These attributes are captured under the general term of *rational economic man* (REM) or *homo economicus*.

REM is an expert in dealing with *utils*. The util is the theoretical unit of measurement of utility, which economists take to mean enjoyment or gratification. Economists often focus on the *change in utility* rather than the amount of utility a person happens to have.

For example, I might have a $20 note in my pocket and an empty stomach. If I see a packed sandwich on sale for $3, I am likely to want to gain some utils by buying and eating the sandwich while at the same time sacrificing some of the utils associated with the $3 I have to fork out. Overall, though, after I eat the sandwich, I am a happier person. A different person, who preferred hunger to paying out, might decide to try and ignore their stomach and hold on to the full $20 note. This person would prefer, and be happier, forgoing food this way.

We say that REM tries to maximise *marginal utility*. Marginal utility is the utility one gets at the margin. It can roughly be taken to mean the utility gained or lost from the last transaction. In our example, the smallest transaction in the circumstances was buying the packed sandwich. I could not buy half a sandwich. So what I tried to do was maximise the utility I derived from the transaction. And so did the more thrifty case who did not buy the sandwich, in their way. Given the circumstances he or she is in, therefore, REM tries to maximise the utility derived from each and every transaction.

Utility theory

Utility theory, of course, does not rely on money for its validity. Money is a convenient medium to have because it can be exchanged for most other things, it is easily portable, and can be divided into very small parts. But the theory works just as well between any other goods; say, the proverbial tractors versus missiles, or apples versus oranges.

There are many interesting economic arguments about the utility of different goods and services. For example, why is water inexpensive when it is so essential but diamonds are so expensive but nonessential? Marginal theory suggests that this is because water is abundant in some parts of the world and getting a litre or losing a litre is not going to make much difference, while finding a diamond or losing one does.[45] Marginal utility theory does not look at the total quantity of water or diamonds available but at what utility is being derived by that particular individual under specific circumstance when there are small changes.

Furthermore, REM is rational because of efficiency (maximum value at the least cost) not moral certitude. Economists do not claim that economic agents are rational because they know what is best for themselves or humanity in the long term but simply that agents know what's best for them when it comes to trading in utils.

Adam Smith, a pioneer of political economy, described *homo economicus* thus:

"It is not from the benevolence of the butcher, the brewer, or the baker that we expect our dinner, but from their regard to their own interest. We address ourselves, not to their humanity but to their self-love, and never talk to them of our own necessities but of their advantages."

The Wealth of Nations

Very often, of course, we cannot be sure of what is going to happen once we decide on a particular course of action. We are often acting under conditions of uncertainty. If I decide to play a game based on the tossing of a fair coin, I know that I have a 50:50 chance of winning or losing. If I stand to win $100 or lose $100 on the toss of a coin, how much can I rationally expect to win? The answer is, of course, zero.

My chance of winning is 50%.
If I win I get $100, which we show as + $100.

My chance of losing is also 50%.
If I lose I have to pay $100, which we show as – $100.

My expectation is therefore
(50% of + $100) plus (50% of – $100) which is + $50 – $50 = 0.

To find *expected utility*, therefore, we multiply the expected utilities of the outcomes by the probabilities of those outcomes and find a weighted average.

---

[45] Economists taking a different approach argue that it is relative scarcity and cost of production which accounts for the difference in price.

I am playing another game. I have a 30% chance of winning $100, a 50% chance of winning $200 and a 20% chance of losing $600. What is my expectation?

(30% of + $100) plus (50% of + $200) plus (20% of – $ 600),

or:

($30) + ($100) + (-$120) = $10

My expected utility is therefore $10 and a REM would play this game because there is a potential gain of $10.

Of course, here too, I am making assumptions. I am assuming that the casino's bank does actually pay if I win $100 or $200. I am assuming that I will pay $600 if I lose. I am also assuming that the probabilities have been properly verified, and that the chances associated with the respective amounts are indeed 30%, 50% and 20%. Often, neither the probabilities nor the payoffs are certain and this compounds the difficulties of making the appropriate decision. When starting a new business, for example, you do not know the payoffs, if any, nor the probabilities of such payoffs, nor, indeed, the timing of the payoffs. The more the uncertainty, the more difficult a decision becomes.

Furthermore, decisions on the probability of different outcomes are often subjective. A pessimist might think the odds for a good payoff are too small while an optimist takes too rosy a view.

However, even if the probabilities were objective, and certain, whether I actually decide to play the game or not depends on my attitude to risk. Do I want to take a 20% risk of losing $600 to have the chance of winning $10? This simple sounding question is one of the pillars of behavioural finance.

Appendix Two –
Table Of Biases

Table of biases

Bias	Nature	Page
Ambiguity aversion	Emotional	84, 85
Anchoring and adjustment	Cognitive	60-3
Availability	Cognitive	52-3
Certainty effect	Emotional	93-4, 100
Change/state	Cognitive	35
Cognitive dissonance	Cognitive	38
Conservatism	Cognitive	75, 88
Confirmation	Cognitive	37-8
Conjunction fallacy	Heuristic driven	46
Disposition effect	Emotional	90-1
Endowment	Emotional	77
Framing	Cognitive	56-8
Frequency/probability	Cognitive	75
Gambler's fallacy	Cognitive	49-51
Hindsight	Cognitive	43-4
Illusion of control	Cognitive	78-9
Isolation effect	Cognitive	33
Loss aversion	Emotional	88-9
Mental accounting	Cognitive	59-60
Noise trading	Heuristic driven	34-5
Optimism/pessimism	Emotional	69-74
Overconfidence	Cognitive	76
Recency	Cognitive	54
Regret aversion	Emotional	86-7
Representativeness	Cognitive	45-6, 50-1, 64
Sample-size neglect	Cognitive	51
Selective perception	Cognitive	37
Self-attribution	Cognitive	78-9
Self-control	Emotional	91
Status quo	Emotional	74-7
Stereotypes	Heuristic driven	34, 45, 63-4
Underreaction/overreaction	Emotional	75

Appendix Three –
MTP Checklist

MTP checklist

Money

- What am I currently getting for my money?

- What other investments can I put my money in?

- How much money can I risk on this deal?

- Can I borrow and what is the cost and terms of leveraging?

- What is the nature of the asset that I am proposing buying?

- How will inflation/deflation affect the asset?

- How liquid is my current/future investment?

Time

- What is my investment horizon?

- How long can I wait at the outside?

- Do I have the time to try and turn a bad short-term investment into a good long-term investment?

- What are the time conditions attached to my borrowings or to my other investments?

- Does the structure of the deal increase or decrease my time flexibility?

Probabilities

- What forces are likely to push prices so that I make a profit on this deal?

- What can go wrong?

- Why does Mr Market want to sell?

- Is Mr Market underestimating the cash flows or overstating the discount rate?

- What are my probabilities of winning on this deal?

- Does the structure of the investment help or hinder my probabilities?

- Will the probabilities have time to work in my favour during my time frame?

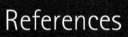

References

Chapter One: The Behavioural Finance Revolution

Richard J. Shiller, 'Human Behavior and the Efficiency of the Financial System,' NBER Working Paper No. W6375, January 1998. This paper gives an interesting introduction to the subject as it was at the time.

Chapter Two: People Acting Strange

Daniel Kahneman at:
nobelprize.org/nobel_prizes/economics/laureates/2002/kahneman-autobio.html

Benedetto De Martino, Dharshan Kumaran, Ben Seymour, Raymond J. Dolan, 'Frames, Biases, and Rational Decision-Making in the Human Brain,' *Science*, August 4, 2006, 313, no. 5787: pp. 684-687.

Paul Slovic, Melissa L. Finucane, Ellen Peters, and Donald G. MacGregor , 'Risk as Analysis and Risk as Feelings: Some thoughts about affect, reason, risk, and rationality,' *Decision Research*, 2002, Oregon.

Jane Spencer, 'Lessons from The Brain-Damaged Investor,' *Wall Street Journal*, July 20, 2005.

Ed Seykota, website www.seykota.com/tribe

Chapter Three: Dealing with Complexity

Werner de Bondt, 'A Portrait of the Individual Investor,' *European Economic Review*, 1998, 42: pp. 831-844.

G. Gigerenzer, 'Ecological Intelligence: An Adaptation for Frequencies,' *The Evolution of Mind*, D. Cummins and C. Allen, eds. (Oxford: Oxford University Press, 1998), pp. 107-125.

B.R. Forer, 'The Fallacy of Personal Validation: A classroom Demonstration of Gullibility,' *Journal of Abnormal Psychology,* 1949, 44: pp. 118-121.

Chapter Four: Perception

Amos Tversky and Daniel Kahneman, 'Extension versus Intuitive Reasoning: the Conjunction Fallacy in Probability Judgement,' *Psychological Review*, 1983, 90.

Werner De Bondt and Richard Thaler: (1) 'Does the Stock Market Overreact?' *Journal of Finance,*1985, 40:793-805; (2) 'Further Evidence on Investor Overreaction and Stock Market Seasonality,' *Journal of Finance*, 1987, 42: pp. 557-581.

Amos Tversky and Daniel Kahneman, 'The Framing of Decisions and the Psychology of Choice,' *Science*, 1981, 211: pp. 453-458.

H. Shefrin and R.H. Thaler ,'The Behavioural Life-Cycle Hypothesis,' *Economic Inquiry,* 1988, printed in R.H. Thaler, *Quasi Rational Economics.*

A. Tversky and D. Kahneman, 'Judgement Under Uncertainty: Heuristics and Biases,' *Science,* 1974, 185: pp. 1124 1131.

Chapter Five: The Self

For studies about financial forecasts and the work of securities analysts and strategists see, for example, two interesting discussions, one in Hersh Shefrin, *Beyond Greed and Fear*, Harvard Business School Press, 2000, Chapters 5 and 18, and the other in, James Montier, *Behavioural Investing: A Practitioners' Guide to Applying Behavioural Finance*, John Wiley & Sons, 2007, Section III.

D. Dreman and M. Berry, 'Analysts Forecasting Errors and Their Implications for Security Analysis,' *Financial Analysts' Journal* 51 (May/June 1995): pp. 30-41.

Chapter Six: Aversion

'Que Sera, Sera', song written by Jay Livingston and Ray Evans.

Sigmund Freud, 'Introductory Lectures'.

Hersh Shefrin and Meir Statman, 'The Disposition to Sell Winners Too Early and Ride Losers Too Long: Theory and Evidence,' *Journal of Finance*, 1985, 40: pp. 777-790.

Daniel Kahneman and Amos Tversky, 'Prospect Theory: An Analysis of Decisions Under Risk,' *Econometrica*, 1979, 47: pp. 313-27.

Joshua D. Coval and Tyler Shumway, 'Do Behavioral Biases Affect Prices?' EFA 2001 Barcelona Meetings, May 4, 2001.

Chapter Seven: Society

Desmond Morris, *The Naked Woman – A Study of the Female Body*, Thomas Dunne Books, St. Martin's Press, 2005, New York, NY.

Kimberlee Weaver, Stephen M. Garcia, Norbert Schwarz, and Dale T. Miller, 'Inferring the Popularity of an Opinion from its Familiarity: A Repetitive Voice can Sound like a Chorus,' *Journal of Personality and Social Psychology*: Vol.92, No.5.

The fascinating subject of smart crowds: Scott E. Page, *The Difference: How the Power of Diversity Creates Better Groups, Firms, Schools, and Societies* (Princeton, NJ: Princeton University Press, 2007); Howard Rheingold, *Smart Mobs: The Next Social Revolution* (Cambridge, MA: Perseus Press, 2002); and, James Surowiecki, *The Wisdom of Crowds: Why the Many are Smarter than the Few and How Collective Wisdom Shapes Business, Economies, Societies, and Nations* (New York: Doubleday and Company, 2004).

Two early books by George Soros: *The Alchemy of Finance*, (John Wiley & Sons, 1994, New York, NY); *Soros on Soros – Staying Ahead of the Curve*, with Byron Wien and Krisztina Koenen, John Wiley & Sons, 1995, New York, NY.

Chapter Eight: Gender

Margo Wilson and Martin Daly, 'Do Pretty Women Inspire Men to Discount the Future?' The Royal Society: Biology Letters, 2003, London, UK.

Brian Knutson, G. Elliott Wimmer, Carmelia M. Kuhnen, Piotr Winkielman, 'Nucleus Accumbens Activation Mediates the Influence of Reward Cues on Financial Risk Taking,' *NeuroReport,* 2008, 19: pp. 509-513.

J.M. Coates, J. Herbert, 'Endogenous Steroids and Financial Risk Taking on a London Trading Floor,' Proceedings of the National Academy of Sciences of the United States of America, April 2008, PNAS 105: pp. 6167-6172.

J.M. Coates, M. Gurnell, A. Rustichini, 'Second-to-Fourth Digit Ratio Predicts Success Among High-Frequency Financial Traders,' Proceedings of the National Association of Science, 2009, 106: pp. 623-628.

James R. Roney, Katherine N. Hanson, Kristina M. Durante, Dario Maestripieri, 'Reading Men's Faces: Women's Mate Attractiveness Judgments Track Men's Testosterone and Interest in Infants,' Proceedings of the Royal Society B: Biological Sciences, May 9, 2006, online publication.

Hessel Oosterbeek, Randolph Sloof, Gijs van de Kuilen, 'Cultural Differences in Ultimatum Game Experiments: Evidence from a Meta-Analysis,' *Experimental Economics*, June 2004, published by Springer Netherlands.

M. Hsu, C. Anen, and S. R. Quartz, 'The Right and the Good: Distributive Justice and Neural Encoding of Equity and Efficiency,' *Science*, May 8, 2008, DOI: 10.1126/science.1153651.

Brad M. Barber, Terrance Odean, 'Boys Will be Boys: Gender, Overconfidence, and Common Stock Investment,' *Quarterly Journal of Economics*, February 2001, 116, no. 1: pp. 261-292.

Chapter Nine: Behavioural Technical Analysis

Warren E. Buffett, Letter to the Shareholders of Berkshire Hathaway Inc., 2007.

Philip A. Fisher, *Common Stocks and Uncommon Profits*, John Wiley & Sons, 1996 (originally published by Harper & Brothers, 1958), New Jersey.

Larry Williams, interview by William M. Caruso, in *Technically Speaking*, Market Technicians Association Inc., Woodbridge, New Jersey, April 2007.

Narasimhan Jegadeesh and Sheridan Titman, 'Returns to buying winners and selling losers: Implications for sock market efficiency', *Journal of Finance*, 1993, 48: pp. 65-91.

Thomas J. George and Chuan-Yang Hwang, 'The 52-week High and Momentum Investing,' *Journal of Finance*, 2004, 59: pp. 2145-2175.

Seung-Chan Park, 'Moving Average Ratio and Momentum,' unpublished manuscript, Millersville University, PA., draft December 2, 2005, available at: www.fma.org/SLC/Papers/movingaverageSeungChanPark.pdf

Chapter Ten: New Horizons

Vaileios Kallinterakis, Mario Pedro Leite Ferreira, 'Herding and Positive Feedback Trading in the Portuguese Stock Exchange: An Exploratory Investigation,' 2007, conferences, Universidade Católica Portuguesa, Porto, Portugal. Paper available at: www.fep.up.pt/conferencias/pfn2006/Conference%20Papers/594.pdf

See also: Vaileios Kallinterakis, Mario Pedro Leite Ferreira, 'Herding and Feedback Trading: Evidence on Their Relationship at the Macro Level,' April 2007. Available at SSRN: ssrn.com/abstract=984681.

William Brock, Josef Lakonishok, and Blake LeBaron, Simple Technical Trading Rules and the Stochastic Properties of Stock Returns,' *The Journal of Finance*, Vol. XLVII, No.5, December 1992.

General references

Adam Smith (George Goodman), *The Money Game*, Michael Joseph Ltd, London.

Peter L. Bernstein, *Against the Gods – The Remarkable Story of Risk*, John Wiley & Sons, 1996, New York, NY.

Richard Bernstein, *Navigate the Noise – Investing in the New Age of Media and Hype*, John Wiley & Sons, 2001, New Jersey.

Barton Biggs, *Hedge Hogging*, John Wiley & Sons, 2006, New Jersey.

Michael Covel, *Trend Following – How Great Traders Make Millions in Up or Down Markets*, Pearson Education Inc, 2004, New Jersey. USA.

Robert D. Edwards, John Magee and W.H.C. Bassetti, *Technical Analysis of Stock Trends*, 8th Edition, CRC Press LLC, 2001, Florida.

Richard Farleigh, *Taming the Lion – 100 Secret Strategies for Investing*, Harriman House Ltd., 2005, Great Britain. (Good insights into the main concepts of investment.)

Max Gunther, *The Zurich Axioms*, Souvenier Press, 1985, London. (A title meant to sound mysterious but a very good book on the right way to approach investment, covering various psychological aspects in a practical way.)

Gustave Le Bon, *The Crowd*, Transaction Publishers, 1995, New Jersey.

Edwin Lefèvre, *Reminiscences of a Stock Operator*, originally published in 1923 by George H. Doran and Company, USA. (A classic detailing the thinking and methods of Jesse L. Livermore.)

Benoit Mandelbrot and Richard L. Hudson, *The (mis)Behavior of Markets – A Fractal View of Risk, Ruin, and Reward*, Basic Books (Perseus Books Group), 2004, New York, NY.

John J. Murphy, *Technical Analysis of the Financial Markets – A Comprehensive Guide to Trading Methods and Applications*, New York Institute of Finance, 1999, New York, NY.

Victor Niederhoffer, *The Education of a Speculator*, John Wiley & Sons, 1997, New Jersey.

Michael M. Pompian, *Behavioural Finance and Wealth Management – How to Build Optimal Portfolios That Account for Investor Biases*, John Wiley & Sons, 2006, New Jersey.

Robert Rhea, *The Dow Theory*, originally published by Barron's, 1932, USA.

Richard Russell, *The Dow Theory Today*, originally published by Richard Russell Associates and Barron's, 1958, New York, NY.

George Soros, *The Crisis Of Global Capitalism: Open Society Endangered*, Public Affairs (Perseus Books Group), 1998, New York, NY.

Lucius Anneeus Seneca, *Letters from a Stoic: Epistulae Morales ad Lucilium*, Penguin Books, 2004, London.

Nassim Nicholas Taleb, *Fooled by Randomness*, originally published by Texere Publishing, 2001, USA.

Index

A

ambiguity aversion 84, 85, 141

amygdala 22, 23, 106

anchoring and adjustment 60, 63, 75, 76, 141, 161

anterior cingulate cortex (ACC) 23

ascending triangle 110-11

availability 52-3, 55, 64, 141, 146, 148

aversion 9-10, 83-100

    ambiguity 84-5, 141

    investing, and, 99-100

    loss 88-9, 141, 154

    regret 86-7, 99

    risk 124, 126, 127

B

Barber, Brad M. 127-8

barn door closing 38

behavioural technical analysis xiii, 79, 135, 161, 168-170

Bernstein, Richard 58

bias 18-19

Biggs, Barton 36

bounded rationality 7-8

broadcning formations 109 110, 112,

Buffett, Warren E. 81, 137

Buridan's donkey 21-2

C

certainty effect 93-4, 100

change/state 35

Claparede, Edward 22

Coates, J. M. 123-4

cognitive bias 43-4

cognitive dissonance 38

comparisons 44-5, 63, 64

confirmation 37-8

conversion 143-5, 148, 163

conjunction fallacy 46

conservatism 75, 76, 77, 88, 155, 156, 157

contrarians 135, 142, 143-5

cortisol 124

Covel, Michael 147

CPA-SSG framework 9

D

Daly, Martin 121-2

Damasio, Antonio 22

data 34-5

De Bondt, Werner 34, 49

decision paralysis 77, 79

descending triangle 109-110

V

value function 95-9

value investing 70-1

       versus growth investing 70

vested interest 77, 79

virtuous (vicious) spiral 103, 115, 118

W

Williams, Larry 147

Wilson, Margo 121, 122

wisdom 34, 38, 148

wishful thinking 31, 37, 39, 99

withdrawal 31, 33, 36

Lightning Source UK Ltd.
Milton Keynes UK
UKHW050636080822
406989UK00004B/216